MATHEMATICS
REVISION GUIDE
FOR

PMB

Penilaian Menengah Bawah

John Suffolk and
Dr Hjh Zaitun bte Hj Taha

MACMILLAN

Contents ——————————————

1   The PMB Mathematics Examination   *1*

2   Whole Numbers and Integers   *4*

3   Fractions and Decimals   *11*

4   Percentages and Everyday Mathematics   *21*

5   Indices and Standard Form   *27*

6   Rate, Ratio and Proportion   *33*

7   Measures   *38*

8   Area   *44*

9   Surface Area and Volume   *49*

10   Introduction to Algebra   *53*

11   Algebraic Expressions and Formulae   *58*

12   Simultaneous Equations and Inequalities   *64*

13   Coordinates and Graphs   *69*

14   Angles and Polygons   *78*

15   Congruence and Similarity   *86*

16   Symmetry and Transformation Geometry   *92*

17   Circles   *101*

18   Pythagoras' Theorem and Trigonometry   *106*

19   Introduction to Statistics   *114*

Answers   *122*

Unit 1
THE PMB MATHEMATICS EXAMINATION

This revision guide is designed to help you to do as well as possible in the Penilaian Menengah Bawah Mathematics Examination of the Board of Examinations, Ministry of Education, Brunei Darussalam.

Revising for the examination

This book contains sections reviewing all the material that is included in the form 3 examination. Read through each section carefully and work through the exercise at the end of the section.

Just reading your exercise book and a textbook is not a good way of revising. You will learn very little if your revision is passive and not active. **It is important that you solve many exercises when revising mathematics.** Doing these exercises will tell you whether you have understood the topic fully. If you have not, you should go back and read through the topic again.

To revise a topic in this book

1. **Read through a section**. Try to identify the important information in the section. Then close the book and try to write down the important information. Then open the book and compare what you have written with what is in the book. If you are mostly correct, work though the examples.
2. **Work through the examples**. When you come to an example
   (i) Try to do it before reading the solution in the book.
   (ii) If you cannot do it, read through the solution in the book. Then try it again without looking in the book.
3. Do the **exercise** for the topic.
4. Do some questions on the topic from **past papers**. But do not do them until you have revised the topic.

The examination

There are **two** examination papers.

Paper 1 lasts for $1\frac{1}{2}$ hours and contains 25 short questions. Each question has two parts. So there are 50 answers to be given. Each question part carries the same number of marks. **Answer all the questions on the paper.**

1

In this paper you are **not** allowed to use a calculator.

Paper 2 lasts for 2 hours. The questions in this paper are longer than those in Paper 1. This paper is in two sections:

- Section A consists of 5 questions with many parts. **You have to answer all these questions.**
- Section B contains 6 questions. **You have to answer ANY FOUR questions from this section.**

In this paper you **are** allowed to use a calculator. It is better to have a good, scientific calculator than a simple four-function one.

In Section B, you should choose the four questions that you can get the most marks for. Read through all the questions before you choose which four you are going to do. You should do this during the **5 minutes reading time** at the start of the examination.

Do not answer more than four questions. Do not think that the examiners will mark all your questions and choose the best four marks. It is often the practice to mark the first four questions and ignore the rest.

Look at past papers to make sure that you are familiar with the way the examinations are organised.

The day before the examination

Make sure that you get plenty of **sleep** the night before the exam. You want to come into the exam hall feeling awake and able to do your best.

Make sure that you are familiar with the calculator that you are going to use in Paper 2. If you use an unfamiliar calculator, there may be some feature that you do not understand how to use – and you are not allowed to take the manual into the exam hall!

Answering the examination questions

If you follow this advice, you should be able to do your best in the exam.

1. **At the start of the exam**, write down all the formulae that are not stated on the exam paper that you may need on the exam. It is very easy to forget these when under the pressure of answering a question. Read through the paper carefully. Underline the important words in each question.

2. **Time** is important in exams. Use the limited time in the examination in the most effective way.
   - (a) **Never spend too long on a question.** There are many easy questions later in the paper. You can pick up many marks from them. If you spend too much time on the earlier questions, you won't have time to get to them.
   - (b) You may find that you are not able to finish the whole paper. In this case, you need to try to get as many marks as possible. When there are

about 20 minutes left, look through the questions that remain to be done, pick out the easiest parts and do them first.

(c) There are no extra marks for finishing early. If you do finish early, use the time to go through your paper and check your answers. Check whether you have made any careless mistakes.

(d) **Do the easiest problems first**. If you cannot do a question – do not panic! Go on to the next question, and come back to it when you have finished the other questions. Examinations can be very frightening, but they can be beaten. It is easy to panic or to get stuck on questions and not to do as well as you had expected.

(e) **In Paper 2**, some questions are worth more marks than others are. Do not spend too long on a question that carries few marks.

3. **Present your work well.**

(a) Set out your work **neatly and legibly**. If your work is messy, it is easy for you to misread your working and get the answer wrong. It is also hard for the examiner to understand your working and give marks for the use of a correct method. The examiner cannot give you marks if your writing cannot be read!

(b) If you cannot finish a question, **do not cross out the work** that you have done; it may earn some marks. In any question, do what you can and you may pick up some marks.

(c) **Do all your working in the space provided on the answer paper** next to the question. Sometimes marks are awarded for being partially correct. If all your working is somewhere else the examiner will not be able to see it.

4. **Some tips to help you with the maths:**

(a) When answering a question, read it carefully and ask yourself these questions: What information is in the question? What am I being asked to work out? What formula do I need? Write the formula down as you have remembered it, and then substitute numbers in it.

(b) If it is a question about **angles** on a figure, and you cannot immediately see what the answer is, write all the angles you can on the figure. Often the answer to the question will then be easier to see.

(c) Make a **rough estimate** of the answer to calculation questions. This will help you check your calculations.

(d) The **units** to be used in the answers are usually stated in the answer space. Make sure that you use the same units in your working.

(e) Make sure that you give your answer to the required amount of **accuracy** – the correct number of decimal places or significant figures. However, when solving a problem, do not approximate **too early** as this can change your answer too much.

Unit 2
WHOLE NUMBERS AND INTEGERS

Basic arithmetic – order of operations, including brackets

$4 + 5 - 3 \times 12 \div 4$ has four operations in it. In what order should they be done?

Addition, subtraction, multiplication and division should always be carried out in the same order. The order is summarised as BODMAS.

EXAM TIP

BODMAS is short for **B**rackets, **O**f, **D**ivision, **M**ultiplication, **A**ddition, **S**ubtraction.
1. Work out Brackets first
2. Then, work out 'Of'
3. Next, do Division and Multiplication, **working from left to right**
4. Finally, do Addition and Subtraction, **working from left to right**

For example,
$$4(5+2) = 4 \times 7 = 28 \qquad 8 \div 4 + 4 = 2 + 4 = 6 \qquad 8 - 4 \div 2 = 8 - 2 = 6$$

When division and multiplication are together, work from left to right:
$$8 \div 4 \times 2 = 2 \times 2 = 4 \qquad 8 \div 4 \div 2 = 2 \div 2 = 1$$
When addition and subtraction are together, work from left to right.
BODMAS is NOT an instruction to do addition before subtraction.
$$8 - 4 + 2 = 4 + 2 = 6 \qquad 7 - 3 - 2 = 4 - 2 = 2$$

$8 \div \frac{2}{3}$ of $12 = 8 \div 8 = 1$ $60 + 12 \times 9 \div (8 - 2 \times 3) = 60 + 12 \times 9 \div (8 - 6)$
(Do 'of' first) $$= 60 + 12 \times 9 \div 2$$
$$= 60 + 54 = 114$$

The operations under or over a division line should be done first.

(a) $32/4 + 6 = \dfrac{32}{4} + 6$

            $= 8 + 6 = 14$

(b) $\dfrac{7+5}{4} - \dfrac{13-9}{2} = \dfrac{12}{4} - \dfrac{4}{2}$

                                 $= 4 - 2 = 2$

Factors and multiples

There are several different kinds of numbers.

The **natural** numbers are 1, 2, 3, 4, 5, ...
The **whole** numbers are 0, 1, 2, 3, 4, ...
The **integers** are ..., $-3, -2, -1, 0, 1, 2, 3, ...$
Rational numbers are of the form p/q, with p and q integers and $p \neq 0$; these are *fractions*.

The **square** numbers are: 1, 4, 9, 16, 25, 36, 49, 64, 81, ... They are called square numbers because they are the areas of 1 by 1, 2 by 2, 3 by 3, 4 by 4, ... squares.
Using a calculator: to find 18^2, type 18, INV, x^y, 2, = and read the answer 324.

The cube numbers are 1, 8, 27, 64, 125, 216, ... They are called cubes because they are the volumes of 1 by 1 by 1, 2 by 2 by 2, 3 by 3 by 3, ... cubes.
Using a calculator: to find 27^3, type 27, INV, x^y, 3, = and read the answer 19 683.

Prime numbers are natural numbers that are only divisible by *exactly* two different natural numbers, themselves and 1. The primes are 2, 3, 5, 7, 11, 13, ...
  1 is only divisible by itself; it is not prime.
  14 is divisible by another natural number, 2, so it is not a prime number. It is a **composite** number. The composite numbers are 4, 6, 8, 9, 10, 12, 14, 15, 16, 18, 20, ...
  Composite numbers are sometimes called rectangular numbers as they can be shown as rectangles. For example:

$$
\begin{array}{l}
x \ \ x \ \ x \ \ x \ \ x \qquad 10 = 2 \times 5 \\
x \ \ x \ \ x \ \ x \ \ x
\end{array}
$$

The **factors** of a number divide exactly into the number. (Do not confuse **factors** and **fractions** – similar sounding words but they have quite different meanings.)

Example   Find all the factors of 30.

Write down all the products of two natural numbers that make 30:
$30 = 1 \times 30$, $30 = 2 \times 15$, $30 = 3 \times 10$, $30 = 5 \times 6$, $30 = 6 \times 5$.
No need to continue.
The factors of 30 are 1, 2, 3, 5, 6, 10, 15, 30.
The prime factors of 30 are 2, 3 and 5.

Any natural number can be expressed in terms of its prime factors.

For example, $220 = 2 \times 2 \times 5 \times 11$

$ = 2^2 \times 5 \times 11$

This is worked out by repeatedly dividing 220 by the prime numbers, starting with 2.

$$\begin{array}{r|r} 2 & 220 \\ 2 & 110 \\ 5 & 55 \\ 11 & 11 \\ & 1 \end{array}$$

This can also be done with a **factor tree**:
To keep dividing 360, for example, takes a long time. A quicker method is to express 360 as a product, for example as 36×10 and then repeat until all the numbers are prime.

So $360 = 2 \times 2 \times 2 \times 3 \times 3 \times 5$

The Highest Common Factor (H.C.F.) of two or more numbers is the largest number that divides exactly into both or all of them.

The factors of 24 are 1, 2, 3, 4, 6, 8, 12 and 24.
The factors of 36 are 1, 2, 3, 4, 6, 9, 12, 18 and 36.
The common factors are 1, 2, 3, 4, 6, 12. The H.C.F. of 24 and 36 is 12.

The multiples of a number are its times table.
The multiples of 8 are 8, 16, 24, 32, 40, … They are found by **multiplying** 8 by 1, 2, 3, …
The lowest common multiple (L.C.M.) of two numbers is the smallest number that is a multiple of both of them.

Finding the L.C.M. by looking at lists of multiples

Example 1   Find the L.C.M. of 6 and 9.
Write down the multiples of the larger number, 9, and pick out the multiples of 6:
9 has multiples 9, 18, 27, 36, …   18 and 36 are both multiples of 6
The lowest of these is 18. Therefore, 18 is the L.C.M. of 6 and 9.

Example 2   What are the H.C.F. and the L.C.M. of 36 and 72?
$36 \times 2 = 72$, so 72 is a multiple of 36. Therefore, 36 is a factor of 72.
So the H.C.F. of 36 and 72 is 36 and their L.C.M. is 72.

When one of two numbers is a multiple of the other, then their H.C.F. is the **smaller** number. Their L.C.M. is the **larger** of the two numbers.

Finding the L.C.M. by repeated division

Example   Find the L.C.M. of 48 and 72.
Think of a common factor of 48 and 72.

6 is a common factor; divide it into both of them:
$$6 \underline{\lfloor 48 \qquad 72}$$
$$8 \qquad 12$$

Then divide by a common factor of 8 and 12, which is 4:
$$6 \underline{\lfloor 48 \qquad 72}$$
$$4 \underline{\lfloor 8 \qquad 12}$$
$$2 \qquad 3$$

2 and 3 have no common factors, so you cannot divide again.
The L.C.M. is the product of the numbers around the side $= 6 \times 4 \times 2 \times 3$
$= 144$.
You do not need to divide by the smallest prime number each time.
(The H.C.F. is the product of the common factors, $6 \times 4 = 24$.)

Integers: order, addition and subtraction

Integers can be shown on a number line:

Integers have a **direction** shown by the sign: **positive** to the **right**, **negative** to the **left** of **zero**. They have a numerical part. In $^-8$, the sign is negative, the numerical part is 8.

Order

The numbers to the right on the number line are the larger numbers. So $7 > 4$. Also $^-25 < 0$. This statement can be interpreted as '$^-25°C$ is colder than $0°C$', or 'having a debt of \$25 means you are poorer than a person with no debts', and so on.

Negative number plus positive number

Adding a positive number is a move to the right on the number line. Adding a negative number is a move to the left.
For example, $(^-4) + (^+6)$: $(^-4)$ is 4 steps to the left of 0. $+ (^+6)$ is a move of 6 steps to the right. 4 left then 6 right is 2 right. On the number line:

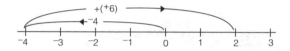

$(^+6) + (^-4)$ has the same answer: 6 right, then 4 left, the result is 2 right $(^+2)$.
So $(^-4) + (^+6) = (^+6) + (^-4) = 6 - 4 = (^+2)$

Another example: $(^-7) + (^+4)$: 7 left, then 4 right is 3 left. On the number line:

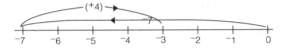

$(^-7) + (^+4) = (^+4) + (^-7) = (^-3)$

Notice the pattern: $(^+5) + (^-4) = (^+1)$ and $(^-7) + (^+4) = (^-3)$
The numerical result is the difference between the numerical parts ($5 - 4 = 1$, $7 - 4 = 3$).
The sign of the answer is the sign in front of the larger numerical part, $^+5$ and $^-7$.

Similarly, $(^-87) + (^+91) = 91 - 87 = ^+4$:   87 left, then 91 right; result is 4 right

$(^-203) + (^+201) = 201 - 203 = ^-2$:   203 left, then 201 right; result is 2 left.

$(^-4) + (^+4) = 0$ So $^-4$ is the **additive inverse** of $^+4$.
$^+6$ is the additive inverse of $^-6$.

The sum of a number and its inverse is 0.	$(^+18) + (^-18) = 0$

Negative number plus negative number

For example, $(^-4) + (^-5) = ^-9$: 4 left and then 5 left is 9 left.
The result of adding two negative numbers is negative. The sum of the numbers is the sum of the numerical parts.
For example, $(^-107) + (^-91) = ^-198$

Subtraction

$(^-4) - (^-4) = 0$ because any number minus itself $= 0$
However $(^-4) + (^+4) = 0$
So $- (^-4)$ has the same effect as $+ (^+4)$
$48 - 48 = (^+48) - (^+48) = 0$ and
$48 + (^-48) = (^+48) + (^-48) = 0$ and $- 48 = + (^-48)$

To subtract an integer, add its inverse.

For example, $(^-6) - (^-8) = (^-6) + (^+8) = ^+2$
$(^-8) - (^+4) = (^-8) + (^-4) = ^-12$

8

Multiplying and dividing integers

Multiplication

($^+$8) × ($^+$5) is the same as 8 × 5 = 40.

By repeated addition, ($^+$5) × ($^-$8) = 5 × ($^-$8)

$$= (^-8) + (^-8) + (^-8) + (^-8) + (^-8)$$
$$= ^-40$$

A positive number times a negative number is negative.

Also, ($^-$8) × ($^+$5) = ($^+$5) × ($^-$8) = $^-$40.

Negative × positive is negative.

Suppose that a book loses $2 in value each year.

In 3 years' time ($^+$3), the book will be worth $6 less. So ($^+$3) × ($^-$2) = $^-$6

Three years ago ($^-$3), the book was worth $6 more (+). So ($^-$3) × ($^-$2) = $^+$6, a positive number.

Negative × negative = positive.

For example, ($^-$8) × ($^-$4) = ($^+$32)   ($^-$6)^2 = ($^-$6) × ($^-$6) = ($^+$36)

EXAM TIP

Remember these rules:
   negative × positive = positive × negative = negative
   positive × positive = negative × negative = positive

Division

Since ($^-$8) × ($^-$4) = ($^+$32), ($^+$32) ÷ ($^-$8) = ($^-$4)

Positive ÷ negative = negative.

Since ($^-$8) × ($^+$4) = ($^-$32), ($^-$32) ÷ ($^+$8) = ($^-$4)

              and   ($^-$32) ÷ ($^-$8) = ($^+$4)

Negative ÷ positive = negative   and   negative ÷ negative = positive

---

EXAM TIP

Remember these rules:
   negative ÷ positive = positive ÷ negative = negative
   positive ÷ positive = negative ÷ negative = positive

Example Evaluate (a) ($^-$8) × ($^-$4) − ($^-$9) × ($^-$6) (b) ($^-$5)^2 − ($^-$6)^2

(a) ($^-$8) × ($^-$4) − ($^-$9) × ($^-$6) = ($^+$32) − ($^+$54) = $^-$22

(b) ($^-$5)^2 − ($^-$6)^2 = ($^+$25) − ($^+$36) = $^-$11

WHOLE NUMBERS AND INTEGERS – TYPICAL QUESTIONS

1 Evaluate
   (a) $40 \div \frac{2}{3}$ of 30   (b) $64 - 12 + 18$ (c) $40 + 20 \times 5 \div (12 - 7)$
   (d) $10 + 4 \times 9 \div 3$ (e) $[\, ^-32 - (^-4) \,] \div 7$ (f) $64 + 14 \times 4 \div (10 - 2)$

2 (a) Find the L.C.M. of   (i) 16 and 20   (ii) 4, 5 and 6   (iii) 18 and 24.
   (b) Find the H.C.F. of   (i) 18 and 30   (ii) 80, 100 and 180
        (iii) 25 and 36.

3 (a) Find the product of 12 and 16.
        Find the product of the H.C.F. and the L.C.M. of 12 and 16.
        What do you notice?
   (b) Find the product of 15 and 24.
        Find the product of the H.C.F. and the L.C.M. of 15 and 24.
        What do you notice?

4 Use a calculator to work out
   (a) 181^2 (b) 17^3 (c) 8^4 (d) 3^8 (e) $4^5 - 5^4$

5 Evaluate
   (a) $(^-5) \times (^-3)$ (b) $(^-8) \div (^-4)$ (c) $(^-5)^2 + (^-3)^3$
   (d) $(^-2)^3 + (^-3)^2$ (e) $(^-4)^2 - (^-2)^3$ (f) $(^-1)^5 + (^-2)^4$

6 Work out
   (a) $(^-4) - (^-5)$ (b) $(^-6) + (^+8)$ (c) $2 - (^-8)$
   (d) $48 - 84$ (e) $(^-8) \, \{(^-5) + (^+3)\}$ (f) $\dfrac{(^-3) \times (^-4)}{(^-3) - (^-4)}$

7 What symbol (<, = or >) should go in each of these boxes to make a true
   statement?
   (a) $^-26$ $\square$ 5   (b) $16 \div 7$ $\square$ $(4 \times 8) \div (6 + 8)$
   (c) $^-24 \div (8 - 2)$ $\square$ $^-4$ (d) $^-24$ $\square$ $(^-1)(^-2)(^-3)(^-4)$
   (e) 28 $\square$ $12 \div 7 + 16 \div 7$ (f) $16 \div (^-8) + (^-1)$ $\square$ $^-6$

Unit 3
FRACTIONS AND DECIMALS

Fractions

This rectangle is divided into 6 parts.
It is divided into sixths. Five sixths are shaded.

Five sixths is written as the **fraction** $\frac{5}{6}$. The bottom number, 6, is the **denominator** of the fraction. It is the number of parts into which the rectangle has been divided. The top number, 5, is the **numerator**. It is the number of parts that have been shaded.

6 of these 11 balls are black. $\frac{6}{11}$ of the balls are black.

The stick is divided into 10 sections. $\frac{7}{10}$ of the stick is shaded.

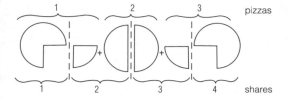

pizzas

3 pizzas are shared by 4 people. Each person gets $\frac{3}{4}$ of a pizza.

shares

Equivalence and order of fractions; proper and improper fractions; mixed numbers

     Folded in 4:

$\frac{1}{2}$ of this rectangle is shaded. $\frac{4}{8}$ is shaded.

In both diagrams, the same amount is shaded. $\frac{1}{2}$ and $\frac{4}{8}$ are **equivalent**, equal fractions.

11

To change $\frac{1}{2}$ into $\frac{4}{8}$, both numerator and denominator are multiplied by 4:

$$\frac{1}{2} = \frac{1 \times 4}{2 \times 4} = \frac{4}{8}$$

To change $\frac{4}{8}$ into $\frac{1}{2}$, both numerator and denominator are divided by 4:

$$\frac{4}{8} = \frac{4 \div 4}{8 \div 4} = \frac{1}{2}$$

$\frac{1}{2}$ of these 8 balls are circled:  $\frac{4}{8}$ are circled.

Another example:

$$\frac{3}{4} = \frac{3 \times 3}{4 \times 3} = \frac{9}{12} \quad \text{and} \quad \frac{9}{12} = \frac{9 \div 3}{12 \div 3} = \frac{3}{4}$$

So $\frac{3}{4}$ and $\frac{9}{12}$ are equivalent, equal fractions.

EXAM TIP

Multiplying or dividing the numerator and denominator of a fraction by the same whole number makes an equivalent fraction.

Dividing the numerator and denominator of the fraction by the same natural number makes a simpler equivalent fraction. When the numerator and denominator can no longer be divided, the fraction is in its **simplest form**.

For example, $\frac{8}{12} = \frac{8^2}{12^3} = \frac{2}{3}$, dividing by 4. $\frac{8}{12}$ in its simplest form is $\frac{2}{3}$.

Example Copy and complete $\frac{3}{5} = \frac{6}{-} = \frac{}{35}$

Write this as two problems: $\frac{3}{5} = \frac{6}{-}$ and $\frac{3}{5} = \frac{}{35}$

Then $\frac{3}{5} = \frac{2 \times 3}{2 \times 5} = \frac{6}{10}$ and $\frac{3}{5} = \frac{3 \times 7}{5 \times 7} = \frac{21}{35}$, so $\frac{3}{5} = \frac{6}{10} = \frac{21}{35}$

Order of fractions

Five eighths is greater than three eighths.

(5 squares are more than 3 squares.)

When fractions have the same denominator, the fraction with the larger numerator is greater.

3/8

5/8

$$\frac{5}{8} > \frac{3}{8}$$

12

To compare two fractions with different denominators, e.g. $\frac{5}{8}$ and $\frac{7}{12}$, change them to equivalent fractions with the same denominator. Multiply the numerator and denominator of each fraction by the denominator of the other:

For $\frac{5}{8}$ the other denominator is 12:
$$\frac{5}{8} = \frac{5 \times 12}{8 \times 12} = \frac{60}{96}$$

For $\frac{7}{12}$ the other denominator is 8:
$$\frac{7}{12} = \frac{7 \times 8}{12 \times 8} = \frac{56}{96} \quad \text{So } \frac{5}{8} \text{ is larger.}$$

This method is used to put fractions in order.

Example Put these fractions in ascending order: $\frac{5}{6}, \frac{3}{4}, \frac{7}{8}, \frac{19}{24}$

('In ascending order' means in order of size, starting with the smallest.)

The L.C.M. of 6, 4, 8 and 24 is 24.

$\frac{5}{6} = \frac{20}{24}, \frac{3}{4} = \frac{18}{24}, \frac{7}{8} = \frac{21}{24}, \frac{19}{24}$ The order is $\frac{18}{24}, \frac{19}{24}, \frac{20}{24}, \frac{21}{24}$ which is $\frac{3}{4}, \frac{19}{24}, \frac{5}{6}, \frac{7}{8}$

('In descending order' means in order of size, starting with the largest.)

Improper fractions have numerators larger than their denominators, for example $\frac{25}{4}$. Change them into mixed fractions by dividing the numerator by the denominator to get the whole number. The remainder is the fraction.

$24 \div 4 = 6$; $25 \div 4$ is 6 and remainder one quarter, so $\frac{25}{4} = 6\frac{1}{4}$.
Similarly, $\frac{87}{10} = 8\frac{7}{10}$.

Adding and subtracting fractions

With the same denominators

For example: $\frac{2}{5} + \frac{1}{5} = \frac{3}{5}$ 2 fifths + 1 fifth = 3 fifths

In the diagram, two fifths and one fifth are shaded, making three fifths shaded altogether. Add the numerators. When subtracting fractions with the same denominator, subtract the numerators:

$\frac{2}{5} - \frac{1}{5} = \frac{1}{5}$ 2 fifths − 1 fifth = 1 fifth

With different denominators

Example 1 Find $\frac{4}{5} + \frac{1}{10}$

First make the denominators the same.

Step 1 The L.C.M. is 10.
$$\frac{4}{5} + \frac{1}{10} = \frac{4 \times 2}{5 \times 2} + \frac{1}{10}$$

Step 2 Add the numerators:
$$\frac{4}{5} + \frac{1}{10} = \frac{8}{10} + \frac{1}{10} = \frac{9}{10}$$

Example 2 Find $\dfrac{5}{6} - \dfrac{3}{8}$

The L.C.M. of 6 and 8 is 24 and $\dfrac{5}{6} - \dfrac{3}{8} = \dfrac{20}{24} - \dfrac{9}{24} = \dfrac{11}{24}$

Mixed numbers

Add whole numbers and fractions separately, e.g.

$3\frac{3}{4} + 8\frac{4}{5} = 11\frac{3}{4} + \frac{4}{5} = 11 + \frac{15}{20} + \frac{16}{20} = 11 + \frac{31}{20} = 11 + 1\frac{11}{20} = 12\frac{11}{20}$ (as $\frac{31}{20} = 1\frac{11}{20}$)

Subtracting is done in the same way: $8\frac{9}{10} - 4\frac{3}{4} = 4 + \frac{9}{10} - \frac{3}{4}$

$$= 4 + \frac{18}{20} - \frac{15}{20} = 4\frac{3}{20}$$

For example, $14\frac{1}{8} - 5\frac{1}{2} = 9 + \frac{1}{8} - \frac{1}{2} = 9 + \frac{1}{8} - \frac{4}{8}$

$9 + \frac{1}{8} - \frac{4}{8}$ is a problem as $\frac{4}{8} > \frac{1}{8}$.

Change it to $8 + \frac{8}{8} + \frac{1}{8} - \frac{4}{8} = 8\frac{5}{8}$

Multiplying and dividing fractions

Fraction of a whole number

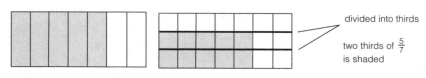

Here are 18 small balls.

$\frac{1}{3}$ of the balls

$\frac{2}{3}$ of the balls

$\frac{1}{3}$ of $18 = \frac{1}{3} \times 18$ is the same as $18 \div 3 = 6$

$\frac{2}{3}$ of $18 = \frac{2}{3} \times 18 = 2 \times 6 = 12$

Another example: $\dfrac{3}{5} \times 50 = \dfrac{3}{\cancel{5}_1} \times \cancel{50}^{10} = 3 \times 10 = 30$

Fraction of a fraction

What is $\frac{2}{3} \times \frac{5}{7}$? The diagrams show $\frac{5}{7}$ and $\frac{2}{3}$ of $\frac{5}{7}$ shaded:

divided into thirds

two thirds of $\frac{5}{7}$ is shaded

$\frac{5}{7}$ shaded $\frac{10}{21}$ shaded   So $\frac{2}{3} \times \frac{5}{7} = \frac{10}{21}$

14

Multiplying fractions: Multiply the numerators together and the denominators together.

For example: $\dfrac{4}{9} \times \dfrac{3}{8} = \dfrac{4 \times 3}{9 \times 8} = \dfrac{12}{72} = \dfrac{1}{6}$

It is often easier to 'cancel' before multiplying: $\dfrac{4}{9} \times \dfrac{3}{8} = \dfrac{4 \times \cancel{3}^1}{\cancel{9}_3 \times 8} = \dfrac{\cancel{4}^1 \times 1}{3 \times \cancel{8}_2} = \dfrac{1}{6}$

Always change **mixed numbers** into improper fractions before multiplying:

$$4\dfrac{1}{2} \times 1\dfrac{1}{3} = \dfrac{\cancel{9}^3}{\cancel{2}_1} \times \dfrac{\cancel{4}^2}{\cancel{3}_1} = 6$$

Dividing

For example: $\quad \dfrac{4}{5} \div \dfrac{2}{3} = \dfrac{\frac{4}{5}}{\frac{2}{3}} = \dfrac{\frac{4}{5} \times \frac{3}{2}}{\frac{2}{3} \times \frac{3}{2}} = \dfrac{\frac{4}{5} \times \frac{3}{2}}{1} = \dfrac{4}{5} \times \dfrac{3}{2}$

So $\quad \dfrac{4}{5} \div \dfrac{2}{3} = \dfrac{4}{5} \times \dfrac{3}{2} = \dfrac{\cancel{4}^2}{5} \times \dfrac{3}{\cancel{2}_1} = \dfrac{6}{5} = 1\dfrac{1}{5}$

$\frac{3}{2}$ is the reciprocal of $\frac{2}{3}$ because $\frac{2}{3} \times \frac{3}{2} = 1$. Any number × its reciprocal is 1.
The reciprocal of $\frac{5}{7}$ is $\frac{7}{5}$: $\quad \frac{5}{7} \times \frac{7}{5} = 1$

To divide a number by a fraction, multiply the number by the reciprocal of the fraction.

For example: $\quad 3\frac{3}{4} \div 2\frac{1}{2} = \frac{15}{4} \div \frac{5}{2} = \frac{15}{4} \times \frac{2}{5} = \frac{3}{2} = 1\frac{1}{2}$

To work out $3\frac{3}{4} \div 2\frac{1}{2}$ on a calculator, enter 3, a^a/c , 3 , a^a/c , 4, ÷, 2, a^a/c, 1, a^a/c, 2, =.

The calculator reads $1\rfloor 1\rfloor 2$ so the answer is $1\frac{1}{2}$

Place value, decimals and fractions

Decimals are another way of writing fractions.

A number with 1 **decimal place (d.p.)** is a fraction with denominator 10:
$0.4 = \frac{4}{10}$

A number with 2 d.p. is a fraction with denominator 100:
$0.36 = \frac{36}{100} \qquad 0.04 = \frac{4}{100}$

A number with 3 d.p. is a fraction with denominator 1000:
$0.384 = \frac{384}{1000} \qquad 0.007 = \frac{7}{1000}$

The number of zeros in the denominator = the number of d.p.

Number	Thousands	Hundreds	Tens	Units	.	Tenths	Hundredths	Thousandths
3020	3	0	2	0				
508.7		5	0	8	.	7		
0.012				0	.	0	1	2
12.098			1	2	.	0	9	8

Each column is one tenth of the column to its left. $1000 \div 10 = 100$, $100 \div 10 = 10$, $10 \div 10 = 1$, $1 \div 10 = \frac{1}{10} = 1$ tenth, 1 tenth $\div 10 = 1$ hundredth, and so on. Numbers on the left of the decimal point are whole numbers. Numbers on the right are decimal fractions.

$$4.8 = 4 + \tfrac{8}{10} \qquad 4.85 = 4 + \tfrac{8}{10} + \tfrac{5}{100} \qquad 4.806 = 4 + \tfrac{8}{10} + \tfrac{0}{100} + \tfrac{6}{1000}$$

Read 0.29 as 'zero point two nine'. Read numbers after the decimal point as single numbers.

Changing fractions to decimals

Change the denominator to a **power** of 10 (powers of 10 are 10, 10^2, 10^3, ...) or divide.

For example: $\quad \dfrac{4}{5} = \dfrac{8}{10} = 0.8 \qquad \dfrac{17}{20} = \dfrac{85}{100} = 0.85$

$$\dfrac{3}{8} = \dfrac{3 \times 125}{8 \times 125} = \dfrac{375}{1000} = 0.375$$

This method can only be used when the denominator is a factor of 10, 100 or 1000. Long division can always be used, e.g. to find $\frac{17}{20}$.

```
       0.85
20 |17.00
   16 0
    1 00
    1 00
       0
```

When changing fractions to decimals, the division either stops or repeats:

```
       0.272...
11 | 3.000
      2 2
        80
        77
        30
        22
```

So $\frac{3}{11} = 0.272727 = 0.\dot{2}\dot{7}$

16

Changing a decimal to a fraction

This follows from the meaning of a decimal, e.g.

$$5.305 = 5\frac{305}{1000} = 5\frac{\cancel{305}^{61}}{\cancel{1000}_{200}} = 5\frac{61}{200}$$

Comparing decimals

Which is more, 0.75 or 0.8? Many students wrongly think that 0.75 is more because 75 is more than 8. But $0.75 = \frac{75}{100}$ and $0.8 = \frac{8}{10} = \frac{80}{100}$ which is greater than $\frac{75}{100}$.

It is not true that the longer a decimal is, the greater it is. If the first d.p. numbers are the same, compare the second d.p. If they are the same, compare the third, and so on. For example, $0.584 > 0.58399$. The first two d.p. are the same. The third d.p. is different, and $4 > 3$.

Rounding to a given number of decimal places and significant figures

4.8 is between 4 and 5; it is nearer to 5 so it is 5 to 1 **significant figure (s.f.)**.
4.2 is also between 4 and 5 but is nearer to 4, so it is 4 to 1 s.f.
4.5 is between 4 and 5 but it is in the middle. We 'round up' and say 4.5 is 5 to 1 s.f.

68.3 is 70 to 1 s.f.	The zero has to be included to show that the 7 is in the tens column.
588 to 1 s.f. is 600	Two zeros are needed to keep the 6 in the hundreds column.
5.88 to 1 s.f. is 6	The zeros are not needed here.
0.0543 is 0.05 to 1 s.f.	The 0 in the tenths column is to keep the 5 in the hundredths column.

EXAM TIP

When the next number is 5 or more, round up. When it is less than 5, round down.

A student works out 48.2×2.152 on his calculator. He says the answer is about 1037. Is this correct? Estimating answers when calculating helps avoid careless mistakes.
To estimate 48.2×2.152, write 48.2 and 2.152 to one significant figure.
48.2 is approximately equal to 50 and 2.152 is approximately equal to 2.
So 48.2×2.152 is approximately $50 \times 2 = 100$, so his answer of 1037 is not sensible.

In the same way   5.88 = 5.9 to 2 s.f.   0.0543 = 0.054 to 2 s.f.
                 6943 is 6940 to 3 s.f.   6999 is 7000 to 3 s.f.

0.05043 = 0.0504 to 3 s.f. The 0 between the 5 and the 4 is significant. Compare it with 504.3 which is 504 to 3 s.f. The number of significant figures is the number of digits from the first non-zero digit to the last non-zero digit, including any zeros in between.

Decimal places

To round a number to 3 decimal places, look at the fourth number. If it is 5 or more then increase the 3rd decimal place number by 1 and leave off the other digits.

4.89876 = 4.899 to 3 d.p. as 7, the 4th decimal (in bold type) is greater than 5.
234.64358 = 234.644 to 3 d.p. as the 4th digit is 5.

The same procedure is used for any number of decimal places:
12.706 = 12.71 to 2 d.p.   8.48802 = 8.4880 to 4 d.p.

Note that 1.996 = 2.00 to 2 d.p. – the zeros must be written in. The answer must always have the number of decimal places that the question asks for.

Adding and subtracting, multiplying and dividing decimals

Adding and subtracting

Decimals are added (and subtracted) in the same way as whole numbers.

$$2.4 + 4.9 = 2\frac{4}{10} + 4\frac{9}{10} = 6\frac{13}{10} = 7\frac{3}{10} = 7.3.$$

$$\begin{array}{cc} 2.4 & 24 \\ +\ 4.9 & +\ 49 \\ \hline 7.3 & 73 \end{array}$$

Compare 24 + 49 = 73.

Add units to units, tenths to tenths and so on. To do this, put the decimal points in line.

For example   3.6 + 14:

$$\begin{array}{r} 3.6 \\ +\ 14 \\ \hline 17.6 \end{array} \qquad 84.2 - 6.3: \qquad \begin{array}{r} 84.2 \\ -\ 6.3 \\ \hline 77.9 \end{array}$$

Multiplying

$3 \times 5 = 15$

one number after decimal point

$$0.3 \times 5 = \frac{3}{10} \times 5 = \frac{3 \times 5}{10} = \frac{15}{10} = 1.5$$

$52 \times 16 = 832$

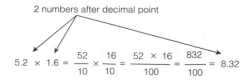

2 numbers after decimal point

$$5.2 \times 1.6 = \frac{52}{10} \times \frac{16}{10} = \frac{52 \times 16}{100} = \frac{832}{100} = 8.32$$

In each case, the number of numbers after the decimal point remains the same.

EXAM TIP

Multiplying decimals: multiply the numbers as if there were no decimal point, then count the number of numbers after the decimal points in the question. The same number of numbers should be after the decimal point in the result of the calculation.

If you work out 4.6×6.5 on a calculator, the answer is 29.9. This appears to break the rule, because there is only one decimal place in the answer. By long multiplication, $4.6 \times 6.5 = 29.90$. There are still two decimal places, but the second one is a 0 and the calculator ignores it.

Example

(a) 8.423×0.9
  $8423 \times 9 = 75\,807$
  $3 + 1 = 4$ numbers after d.p.
  Answer: 7.5807

(b) 1.46×20
  $146 \times 20 = 2920$
  2 numbers after d.p.
  Answer: 29.20, written as 29.2

(c) 14.8×0.35
  $148 \times 35 = 5180$
  $1 + 2 = 3$ numbers after d.p.
  Answer: 5.180 = 5.18

Dividing

$48 \div 1.5 = \frac{48}{1.5}$ Dividing by 1.5 using long division is not easy. Make it easier by changing the divisor to a whole number. Multiply 48 by the same number to keep the answer the same.

$$48 \div 1.5 = \frac{48}{1.5} = \frac{48 \times 10}{1.5 \times 10} = \frac{480}{15} = 32$$

Another example: $0.084 \div 0.24 = \frac{0.084}{0.24} = \frac{0.084 \times 100}{0.24 \times 10} = \frac{8.4}{24} = 0.35$

In this case, the divisor 0.24 has to be multiplied by 100 to remove the decimal point. It does not matter if there is still a decimal in the numerator.

EXAM TIP

Dividing by a decimal: multiply the divisor by a multiple of 10 to make it into a whole number. Multiply the numerator by the same number. Then divide.

19

FRACTIONS AND DECIMALS – TYPICAL QUESTIONS

1 Find three equivalent fractions for each of these.
   (a) $\frac{2}{5}$ (b) $\frac{4}{7}$ (c) $\frac{3}{10}$ (d) $\frac{6}{11}$ (e) $\frac{6}{14}$ (f) $\frac{21}{27}$

2 Express these fractions in their lowest terms.
   (a) $\frac{8}{16}$ (b) $\frac{6}{8}$ (c) $\frac{2}{5}$ (d) $\frac{45}{60}$ (e) $\frac{27}{63}$ (f) $\frac{90}{360}$

3 Complete the following using < or >.
   (a) $\frac{7}{10} \cdots \frac{9}{20}$ (b) $\frac{3}{4} \cdots \frac{2}{3}$ (c) $\frac{4}{5} \cdots \frac{6}{7}$ (d) $\frac{7}{9} \cdots \frac{5}{6}$

4 Write these improper fractions as mixed numbers in their simplest form.
   (a) $\frac{28}{15}$ (b) $\frac{6}{5}$ (c) $\frac{12}{5}$ (d) $\frac{43}{6}$ (e) $\frac{27}{4}$ (f) $\frac{90}{36}$

5 Work these out. Check your answers with a calculator.
   (a) $2\frac{1}{3} + 1\frac{1}{3}$ (b) $\frac{1}{4} + \frac{3}{5}$ (c) $\frac{4}{7} - \frac{2}{5}$ (d) $2\frac{2}{5} - \frac{1}{3}$ (e) $2\frac{1}{2} - 1\frac{2}{5}$

   (f) $3\frac{1}{4} - 1\frac{2}{3} + \frac{1}{4}$

6 Work these out. Check your answers with a calculator.
   (a) $24\frac{1}{2} + 27\frac{1}{3}$ (b) $63\frac{1}{4} + 28\frac{5}{6}$ (c) $14\frac{3}{5} + 26\frac{2}{3}$ (d) $50\frac{3}{4} - 17\frac{1}{8}$

   (e) $124\frac{1}{3} - 6\frac{3}{4}$ (f) $58\frac{1}{4} - 57\frac{3}{4}$

7 Work these out. Check your answers with a calculator.
   (a) $24 - 7\frac{1}{3}$ (b) $64 - 38\frac{3}{4}$ (c) $100 - 26\frac{5}{8}$ (d) $124 - 47\frac{5}{8}$

8 Evaluate the following. Check your answers with a calculator.
   (a) $\frac{2}{5} \times \frac{5}{8}$ (b) $\frac{3}{10} \times \frac{2}{3}$ (c) $1\frac{1}{4} \times \frac{8}{15}$ (d) $2\frac{1}{2} \div \frac{5}{8}$ (e) $1\frac{1}{3} \div 3\frac{1}{7}$

9 Write the following fractions as decimals.
   (a) $\frac{1}{5}$ (b) $\frac{11}{20}$ (c) $\frac{17}{40}$ (d) $\frac{2}{3}$

10 (a) Round 12.542, 10.54, 0.004055 and 1996 to three significant figures.
   (b) Write 43.21, 6.49, 283 456 and 1996 to two significant figures.
   (c) Round 2.04325, 12.555, 4.606 and 1.997 to one decimal place.
   (d) Round 456.7895, 0.01449 and 1.997 to two decimal places.

11 Write
   (a) 42.85 to 1 s.f.   (b) 684 to 2 s.f.   (c) 4.285 to 2 d.p.
   (d) 4.246 to 2 decimal places   (e) 984 423 to 3 s.f.   (f) 0.004234 to 3 s.f.

Unit 4
PERCENTAGES AND EVERYDAY MATHEMATICS

Percentages

A percentage is a **fraction with a denominator of 100**. 'Per cent' means 'out of 100'.

For example, $68\% = \dfrac{68}{100} = \dfrac{17}{25}$

Any percentage can be expressed as a **decimal** by dividing it by 100.

For example, $35\% = \dfrac{35}{100} = 0.35$ (moving each number 2 places to the right).

EXAM TIP

To change a fraction or a decimal to a percentage, multiply the fraction or decimal by 100.

Example Express (a) $\frac{4}{5}$ (b) 0.85 as a percentage.

(a) $\frac{4}{5} = \frac{4}{5} \times 100\% = \dfrac{4 \times 100}{5}\% = 80\%$ (b) $0.85 = 0.85 \times 100\% = 85\%$

Useful percentages:	$50\% = \frac{1}{2} = 0.5$	$25\% = \frac{1}{4} = 0.25$
	$75\% = \frac{3}{4} = 0.75$	$100\% = \frac{100}{100} = 1$
	$33\frac{1}{3}\% = \frac{1}{3} = 0.333\ldots$	$66\frac{2}{3}\% = \frac{2}{3} = 0.666\ldots$
	$10\% = \frac{1}{10} = 0.1$	$20\% = \frac{1}{5} = 0.2$
	$12.5\% = \frac{1}{8}$	$37.5\% = \frac{3}{8}$

Problems involving percentages

Expressing one quantity as a percentage of another

Write one quantity as a fraction of the other, then change it to a percentage.

Example 1 There are 30 students in a class, 12 of them are girls. What is the percentage of boys in the class?

Number of boys = 30 − 12 = 18
Fraction of class who are boys = $\frac{18}{30} = \frac{3}{5}$

Percentage of boys = $\dfrac{\text{Number of boys}}{\text{Total number of students}} \times 100 = \frac{3}{5} \times 100 = 60\%$

> **To find A as a percentage of B, calculate $\dfrac{A}{B} \times 100$**

Example 2 Express 150 m as percentage of 6 km.

Both quantities need to be in the same units. 6 km = 6 × 1000 m = 6000 m
$$\frac{150}{6000} \times 100 = \frac{1}{40} \times 100 = 2.5\%$$

Example 3 I have pocket money of \$3.00 and spent \$0.80 on a drink. What percentage of my money did I spend?

$$\frac{0.80}{3.00} \times 100 = \frac{80}{300} \times 100 = \frac{4}{15} \times 100 = 26.7\% \text{ (to one decimal place)}$$

Finding a percentage of a quantity

Use the same method as for finding a fraction of a quantity.

Example What is 12% of 30 metres of material?

$$12\% \text{ of } 30 \text{ m} = \frac{12}{100} \times 30 \text{ m} = \frac{12 \times 30}{100} \text{ m} = 3.6 \text{ metres}$$

Percentage change

Increases or decreases in quantities such as population are often expressed in percentages.

> **Percentage change $= \dfrac{\text{Change}}{\text{Original amount}} \times 100$**

Example 1 The population of Brunei Darussalam grew from 320 000 to 336 000. What was the percentage increase?

The increase is 336 000 − 320 000 = 16 000

The percentage increase is $\dfrac{16\,000}{320\,000} \times 100\% = \dfrac{\overset{5}{\cancel{16\,000}}}{\underset{1}{\cancel{320\,000}}} \times \cancel{100}\% = 5\%$

In Example 2, we are told the percentage increase and have to work out the new total.

Example 2 This year my father has 8% more fish tanks than last year. Last year he had 50 tanks. How many has he this year?

There are two ways of working this out.

1. 8% of 50 = $\dfrac{8}{100} \times 50 = 4$

   The number of tanks this year = 50 + 4 = 54.

2. If there are 8% more, then the number now is 108% of 50 = $\dfrac{108}{100} \times 50 = 54$.

(If there were 8% **fewer** fish tanks, there would be $(100 - 8)\% = 92\%$ of 50 = 46.)

The change is calculated as a percentage of the original number.

Problems in which you have to find a starting amount

Use a unitary method (see Unit 6 on Rate, ratio and proportion).

Example 1   The number of pupils in a class increased by 20% to 36 pupils. How many pupils were in the class?

A 20% increase means that the number of pupils is 100% + 20% = 120% of the number there was before.

  120% of the previous number is 36

  1% of the previous number is $\dfrac{36}{120}$

  100% of the previous number is $\dfrac{36}{120} \times 100 = 30$. There were 30 pupils.

Example 2   Yesterday I went shopping. I spent 30% of my money and I now have $280 left. How much did I have before I went shopping?

Spending 30% means that I have 100% − 30% = 70% of what I had before.

  70% of my money is $280

  1% of my money is $\$\dfrac{280}{70}$

  100% of my money is $\$\dfrac{280}{70} \times 100 = \$400$. I had $400.

Everyday mathematics

Profit and loss

Percentages are often used in calculations involving money. Normally, people sell goods for more than they paid for them and make a profit. Then:

> **Profit = Selling Price (S.P.) − Cost Price (C.P.)**
>
> **% Profit = $\dfrac{\textbf{Profit}}{\textbf{Cost price}} \times 100$**

Sometimes, people sell things for less than they paid for them and make a loss.

$$\text{Loss} = \text{Cost price} - \text{Selling price}$$
$$\% \text{ Loss} = \frac{\text{Loss}}{\text{Cost price}} \times 100$$

Example 1   Pak Cik Ali bought some durians for $4.00 per kg and sold them for $5.00 per kg. What was his percentage profit?

% profit gained by Pak Ali $= \frac{(\$5.00 - \$4.00)}{\$4.00} \times 100\% = \frac{1}{4} \times 100\% = 25\%$

After 3 days, Pak Ali had some durians left and sold them for $3.50 per kg. What was his percentage loss on these durians?

% loss $= \frac{0.50}{4.00} \times 100\% = \frac{1}{8} \times 100\% = 12.5\%$

Sometimes, the profit and the sale price are known and the cost price has to be calculated.

Example 2   A shop sells a radio for $180 at a profit of 20%. What was the cost price?

The profit is 20%, so the selling price is 100 + 20 = 120% of the cost price.

120% of the cost price $= \frac{120}{100} \times \text{C.P.} = \$180$

So   C.P. $= \$180 \times \frac{100}{120} = \$150$

Discount and commission

Shops often reduce their prices to encourage customers to buy. The reduction is the **discount**.

Example 1   A supermarket is having a sale. All items are being sold at a discount of 30%. What is the sale price of a bag previously sold for $120?

The discount is 30% of $120 $= \frac{30}{100} \times \$120 = \$36$.

The sale price is $120 − $36 = $84.
(Another method: sale price is (100 − 30)% = 70%; 70% of $120 = $84.)

Salespersons are often paid money for each item that they sell. This is called **commission**.

Example 2   Rosmawati sells $1240 worth of cosmetics. Her commission is 5%. How much commission does she get?

She will get 5% of $1240 $= \$\frac{5}{100} \times 1240 = \$62$

Simple interest

Money put in a bank can earn interest. Banks often charge interest for money borrowed from them. The money borrowed or lent is the **principal** (*P*). The **rate** of interest (*R* %) per year (or per annum) is usually written as a percentage. Simple interest is paid once a year.

> **In one year the simple interest paid or earned is $\dfrac{PR}{100}$**
>
> **In *T* years, the simple interest paid or earned is $I = \dfrac{PRT}{100}$**

Example 1　What is the interest paid on a sum of $2000 borrowed for 3 years 6 months at 4%?

Here $P = 2000$, $R = 4$ and $T = 3.5$

$$I = \frac{PRT}{100} = \frac{2000 \times 4 \times 3.5}{100} = 280.$$ The interest is $280.

Example 2　Find the interest rate per annum if the simple interest on a sum of $500 for 2 years is $35.

$P = 500$, $I = 35$ and $T = 2$

$$I = \frac{PRT}{100}, \quad \text{so} \quad 35 = \frac{500 \times R \times 2}{100} = 10R$$

$$R = \tfrac{35}{10} = 3.5 \quad \text{The interest rate is 3.5\%.}$$

Hire purchase

Hire purchase is a system in which a purchaser uses an item before they have finished paying for it. The purchaser pays a deposit and then regular installments until the item is paid for.

Example　A second-hand car is on sale for $7200 cash. Ali agreed to pay 40% of the price as a deposit and then $200 per month for 2 years. How much more does Ali pay for the car by hire purchase than if he had paid cash?

The deposit is 40% of $7200 = $\dfrac{40}{100} \times \$7200 = \$2880$

2 years = 24 months, so Ali also pays $200 × 24 = $4800 in instalments.
Ali pays a total of $2880 + $4800 = $7680.
This is $7680 – $7200 = $480 more than the cash price.

Foreign exchange

Different countries use money with different names and values. When you travel to another country you have to change Bruneian dollars into the currency of that country. The rate at which you change the money is the **exchange rate**. Two examples show how it works.

Example 1   My brother Samri is in the UK. My father is sending him $2500. He changes Brunei dollars into British pounds at the rate of B$1 = GBP 0.38. How many pounds will Samri receive?

My brother receives B$2500 = GBP 2500 × 0.38 = GBP 950

Example 2   My sister comes back from Malaysia with 200 ringgit. If B$1 = MR2.08, how many Brunei dollars does she receive for her ringgit?

MR2.08 = B$1, so MR1 = $$\frac{1}{2.08}$$

My sister has MR200 = $$\frac{1}{2.08} \times 200 = \$96.15$$ to the nearest cent.

PERCENTAGES AND EVERYDAY MATHEMATICS – TYPICAL QUESTIONS

1   (a) Express as percentages: (i) $\frac{7}{10}$ (ii) $\frac{13}{25}$ (iii) $\frac{36}{40}$
    (b) Express as decimals: (i) 78%   (ii) 4.5%   (iii) 245%
    (c) Express as percentages: (i) 0.45   (ii) 2.5   (iii) 0.056
    (d) Express as fractions: (i) 87.5%   (ii) 27.5%   (iii) 275%

2   (a) 15% of a number is 60. Find the number.
    (b) Express 75 km as a percentage of 5000 km.

3   (a) Find the simple interest on $500 borrowed for 3 years at the rate of 12% per annum.
    (b) Calculate the simple interest on $200 at 4% per annum for 5 years.

4   In a school there are 900 boys. 60% of the students are girls. How many girls are in the school?

5   One day the exchange rate between US$ and Brunei dollars was US$1 = B$1.70. Calculate
    (a) the number of Brunei dollars that could be bought for US$230
    (b) the number of US$ that could be bought for B$900.

6   In selling a car for $12 360 the salesman makes a profit of 20%. Find the cost price of the car.

7   The selling price of a computer game was $200. The selling price of the game increased by 20%. What was the new price?

8   During a sale all the prices in a shop were reduced by 15%. A handbag was reduced by $30. Calculate the previous price of the handbag.

9   (a) My family went for a holiday in Malaysia. I changed B$3000 into Malaysian dollars. The exchange rate was B$1 = M$2.40. How many Malaysian dollars did I get?
    (b) I spent M$4000 in Malaysia and changed the rest of my money back to Brunei dollars. The exchange rate was B$1 = M$2.50. How many Brunei dollars did I receive?

Unit 5

INDICES AND STANDARD FORM

Index notation

Indices are a short way of writing products. $2 \times 2 \times 2 \times 2 \times 2 \times 2 \times 2$ is very long.

There are seven 2's multiplied together. In index notation it is written as 2^7 and read as '2 to the power of 7' or '2 to the seventh'. 7 is the **index** and 2 is the **base**.

Five y's multiplied together, $y \times y \times y \times y \times y = y^5$

$5^2 = 5 \times 5 = 25$ is read as '5 squared'
(because 5×5 is the area of a square of side 5 cm).

$6^3 = 6 \times 6 \times 6 = 216$ is read as '6 cubed'
(because $6 \times 6 \times 6$ is the volume of a cube of side 6 cm).

6 cm

$1^3 = 1 \times 1 \times 1 = 1 \qquad 1^n = 1$

Example

(a) $4^2 \times 3^3$

$= 16 \times 27$

$= 432$

(b) $3^3 \div 4^4$

$= \dfrac{27}{256}$

(c) $\dfrac{5^3 \times 4^2}{3^2 \times 2^3}$

$= \dfrac{125 \times 16}{9 \times 8}$

$= \dfrac{250}{9}$

(d) $4^4 - 5^3$

$= 256 - 125$

$= 131$

Square roots and cube roots

8 squared, $8^2 = 8 \times 8 = 64$.

Another way of stating this is to say that a **square root** of 64 is 8.

Since $(^-8) \times (^-8) = 64$, $(^-8)$ is also a square root of 64.

The square roots of 64 are ± 8.

The symbol $\sqrt{}$ is used for the positive square root only. $\sqrt{64} = 8$
(Sometimes this is written $\sqrt[2]{64} = 8$)

Here are some examples:

$10^2 = 100$ so the square roots of 100 are ± 10. $\sqrt{100} = 10$.

4 cubed, $4^3 = 4 \times 4 \times 4 = 64$. The **cube root** of 64 is 4, written: $\sqrt[3]{64} = 4$

To find the square root of any number by using a scientific calculator, type in the number and then press $\sqrt{}$.

The square root of many numbers can be found without a calculator.
For example, since $13^2 = 169$, it follows that

$$\sqrt{1.69} = \sqrt{\frac{169}{100}} = \frac{13}{10} = 1.3$$

This method cannot be used to find $\sqrt{16.9}$ as

$$\sqrt{16.9} = \sqrt{\frac{169}{10}} = \frac{13}{3.162} = 4.11$$

which requires a calculator. The method only works when the numbers are all squares.

Example 1

Find (a) $\sqrt{20\frac{1}{4}}$ (b) $\sqrt{6.25}$ without using a calculator.

(a) $\sqrt{20\frac{1}{4}} = \sqrt{\frac{81}{4}} = \frac{9}{2} = 4\frac{1}{2}$ (b) $\sqrt{6.25} = \sqrt{\frac{625}{100}} = \frac{25}{10} = 2\frac{5}{10} = 2.5$

Example 2 $\sqrt{8.1} = 2.84$. What are $\sqrt{8100}$ and $\sqrt{81\,000}$?

$\sqrt{8100} = \sqrt{81 \times 100} = 9 \times 10 = 90$

$\sqrt{81\,000} = \sqrt{81 \times 10\,000} = 9 \times \sqrt{1000}$

$\sqrt{1000}$ is not a whole number. Use $\sqrt{10\,000} = 100$:

$\sqrt{81\,000} = \sqrt{8.1 \times 10\,000} = 2.84 \times 100 = 284$

EXAM TIP

When solving these sorts of problems, you have to make sure that the power of ten used is a square.
Remember that $10^2 = 100$, $100^2 = 10\,000$, $1000^2 = 1\,000\,000$

Factorising can be used to find the square roots of some larger numbers.
For example, $\sqrt{576}$:

$576 = 4 \times 144 = 4 \times 4 \times 36 = (4 \times 4) \times (6 \times 6) = (4 \times 6) \times (4 \times 6)$

So $\sqrt{576} = 4 \times 6 = 24$

Multiplying numbers in index form

$7^4 \times 7^5 = (7 \times 7 \times 7 \times 7) \times (7 \times 7 \times 7 \times 7 \times 7)$

$\qquad = 7 \times 7 \times 7 \times 7 \times 7 \times 7 \times 7 \times 7 \times 7 = 7^9 = 7^{4+5}$

$9^3 \times 9^2 = (9 \times 9 \times 9) \times (9 \times 9) = 9^5 = 9^{3+2}$

These examples show why $m^a \times m^b = m^{a+b}$

Example Simplify (a) $4^3 \times 4^8$ (b) $5^2 \times 5^3 \times 5^4 \times 5^5$

(a) $4^3 \times 4^8 = 4^{3+8} = 4^{11}$ (b) $5^2 \times 5^3 \times 5^4 \times 5^5 = 5^{2+3+4+5} = 5^{14}$

An expression like $7^4 \times 8^5$ cannot be simplified as the bases 7 and 8 are different.

Dividing numbers in index form – negative and zero indices

$7^5 \div 7^3 = (7 \times 7 \times 7 \times 7 \times 7) \div (7 \times 7 \times 7) = \dfrac{7 \times 7 \times 7 \times 7 \times 7}{7 \times 7 \times 7} = 7^2 = 7^{5-3}$

$9^3 \div 9^2 = \dfrac{9 \times 9 \times 9}{9 \times 9} = 9^1 = 9^{3-2}$

These examples show why $m^a \div m^b = m^{a-b}$

Example 1 Simplify (a) $4^{11} \div 4^6$ (b) $5^8 \div 5^4$

(a) $4^{11} \div 4^6 = 4^{11-6} = 4^5$ (b) $5^8 \div 5^4 = 5^{8-4} = 5^4$

$4^6 \div 4^6 = 4^{6-6} = 4^0$

But $4^6 \div 4^6 = \dfrac{4^6}{4^6} = 1$. So $4^0 = 1$

In the same way, $6^5 \div 6^5 = 6^0 = 1$

For all non-zero a, $a^0 = 1$

$7^4 \div 7^6 = 7^{4-6} = 7^{-2}$

But $7^4 \div 7^6 = \dfrac{7^4}{7^6} = \dfrac{1}{7^2}$. So $7^{-2} = \dfrac{1}{7^2}$

In the same way, $8^{-3} = \dfrac{1}{8^3}$

For all non-zero a, $a^{-n} = \dfrac{1}{a^n}$

Example 2 Find (a) 4^{-3} (b) 51^0

(a) $4^{-3} = \dfrac{1}{4^3} = \dfrac{1}{64}$ (b) $51^0 = 1$

Index rules to remember

1. $m^a \times m^b = m^{a+b}$

2. $m^a \div m^b = m^{a-b}$

3. $(m^a)^b = m^{ab}$

4. $1^n = 1$

5. $a^0 = 1$

6. $a^{-n} = \dfrac{1}{a^n}, a \neq 0$

7. $\left(\dfrac{a}{b}\right)^n = \dfrac{a^n}{b^n}$

8. $a^{1/2} = \sqrt{a}$

9. $a^{\frac{1}{n}} = \sqrt[n]{a}$

10. $a^{\frac{m}{n}} = \sqrt[n]{a^m}$

Example 3 Solve the equation $27^{3x} = 81$

Both 27 and 81 are powers of 3: $27 = 3^3$, $81 = 3^4$

So $(3^3)^x = 3^4$ and so $3^{3x} = 3^4$. Comparing indices, $3x = 4$ and $x = \frac{4}{3} = 1\frac{1}{3}$

Example 4 Find the value of $(8^2)^3 \times (4^{-2})^4$

$(8^2)^3 \times (4^{-2})^4 = (64)^3 \times \dfrac{1}{(4^2)^4}$

$= (64)^3 \times \dfrac{1}{16^4} = \dfrac{64 \times 64 \times 64}{16 \times 16 \times 16 \times 16} = 4$

Powers of numbers in index form

$(7^2)^3 = 7^2 \times 7^2 \times 7^2 = 7^{2+2+2} = 7^6 = 7^{\,2 \times 3}$

$(8^3)^4 = 8^3 \times 8^3 \times 8^3 \times 8^3 = 8^{3+3+3+3} = 8^{12} = 8^{\,3 \times 4}$

These examples show why $(m^{\,a})^b = m^{\,a\,b}$

Fractional indices

$4^{\frac{1}{2}} \times 4^{\frac{1}{2}} = 4^{\frac{1}{2}+\frac{1}{2}} = 4^1 = 4$

But $\sqrt{4} \times \sqrt{4} = 4$, so $4^{\frac{1}{2}} = \sqrt{4}$.   So $a^{\frac{1}{2}} = \sqrt{a}$ for any a that is not negative.

$8^{\frac{1}{3}} + 8^{\frac{1}{3}} + 8^{\frac{1}{3}} = 8^{\frac{1}{3}+\frac{1}{3}+\frac{1}{3}} = 8^1 = 8$

So $8^{\frac{1}{3}} = \sqrt[3]{8} = 2$

In the same way, $81^{\frac{1}{4}} = \sqrt[4]{81} = 3$. So $a^{\frac{1}{n}} = \sqrt[n]{a}$ for any a that is not negative.

Because $(a^m)^n = a^{\,mn}$, $4^{\frac{3}{2}} = (4^{\frac{1}{2}})^3 = 2^3 = 8$

$$27^{-\frac{2}{3}} = \frac{1}{(27)^{\frac{2}{3}}} \quad \text{because } a^{-n} = \frac{1}{a^n}$$

$$= \frac{1}{(27^{\frac{1}{3}})^2} = \frac{1}{3^2} = \frac{1}{9}$$

Example Simplify (a) $64^{\frac{5}{3}}$ (b) $36^{-\frac{3}{2}}$ (c) $\left(\dfrac{4}{9}\right)^{-\frac{3}{2}}$

(a) $64^{\frac{5}{3}} = (64^{\frac{1}{3}})^5 = 4^5 = 1024$

(b) $36^{-\frac{3}{2}} = \dfrac{1}{36^{\frac{3}{2}}} = \dfrac{1}{(36^{\frac{1}{2}})^3} = \dfrac{1}{6^3} = \dfrac{1}{216}$

(c) $\left(\dfrac{4}{9}\right)^{-\frac{3}{2}} = \left(\dfrac{9}{4}\right)^{\frac{3}{2}} = \left(\dfrac{3}{2}\right)^3 = \dfrac{27}{8} = 3\dfrac{3}{8}$

Indices also can be used to find the square roots of some larger numbers.

For example, $784 = 2^4 \times 7^2$ so $\sqrt{784} = 784^{\frac{1}{2}} = (2^4 \times 7^2)^{\frac{1}{2}} = 2^2 \times 7 = 28$

Standard form

The population of Brunei Darussalam in 2001 was 338 000, a large number.

$$338\ 000 = 338 \times 1000 = 338 \times 10^3$$
$$= 3.38 \times 100\ 000 = 3.38 \times 10^5$$

3.38×10^5 is called the **standard form** of 338 000.

In standard form (sometimes called scientific notation), a number is written in the form $a \times 10^n$, where $1 \le a < 10$.

For large numbers, n will be a positive whole number.

For very small numbers, n will be a negative integer.

For example, $0.084 = 8.4 \div 100 = 8.4 \times \dfrac{1}{10^2} = 8.4 \times 10^{-2}$

Example 1 Write these numbers in full.

(a) 4.8×10^3 (b) 2.652×10^4 (c) 5.44×10^{-3} (d) 7×10^{-2}

(a) $4.8 \times 10^3 = 4.8 \times 1000 = 4800$

(b) $2.652 \times 10^4 = 2.652 \times 10\ 000 = 26\ 520$

(c) $5.44 \times 10^{-3} = 5.44 \times \dfrac{1}{1000} = 0.00544$

(d) $7 \times 10^{-2} = 7 \times \dfrac{1}{100} = 0.07$

EXAM TIP

Each figure moves the same number of places as the power of ten in the standard form of the number. If the power is positive, each figure moves to the left. If the power is negative, each figure moves to the right.

Example 2 Evaluate these expressions, leaving the answer in standard form.

(a) $7.6 \times 105 - 240\ 000$ (b) $\dfrac{4.5 \times 10^7}{3 \times 10^3}$ (c) $\dfrac{7.7 \times 10^5}{1.1 \times 10^{-4}}$

(a) $7.6 \times 105 - 240\ 000 = 760\ 000 - 240\ 000 = 520\ 000 = 5.2 \times 105$

(b) $\dfrac{4.5 \times 10^7}{3 \times 10^3} = \dfrac{4.5}{3} \times 107{-}3 = 1.5 \times 104$

(c) $\dfrac{7.7 \times 10^5}{1.1 \times 10^{-4}} = 7 \times 105 - (-4) = 7 \times 10\ 9$

Indices and the calculator

$8^5 = 8 \times 8 \times 8 \times 8 \times 8$ can be calculated on a calculator by repeated multiplication, but that is a waste of time. Just type in 8, y^x, 5, = and read off 32 768. If you work out $81^{-\frac{1}{2}}$ on a calculator, you should get the answer 0.11111... To find the fraction, press 1/x and read off 9. The answer is $\frac{1}{9}$.

INDICES AND STANDARD FORM – TYPICAL QUESTIONS

1 Work out (a) $4^2 \times 5^3$ (b) $4^3 \div 16^2$ (c) $\dfrac{8^3 \times 9^2}{3^3 \times 2^5}$ (d) $3^6 - 6^3$

2 Work out these without a calculator.

(a) $\sqrt{30\frac{1}{4}}$ (b) $\sqrt{2\frac{7}{9}}$ (c) $\sqrt{2.25}$ (d) $\sqrt{3\frac{6}{25}}$

(e) $\sqrt{1296}$ (b) $\sqrt{484}$ (c) $\sqrt{14\,400}$ (d) $\sqrt{900}$

3 $\sqrt{1.6} = 1.26$ to 2 decimal places. What is the value of $\sqrt{160}$?

4 Simplify

(a) $4^5 \times 4^7$ (b) $4^1 \times 4^3 \times 4^5$ (c) $2^3 \times 2^{12}$ (d) $5^8 \div 5^6$

(e) $12^{14} \div 12^{10}$ (f) $5^{17} \div 5^8$ (g) 3^{-2} (h) 6^{-1}

(i) 511^0 (j) $64^{\frac{4}{3}}$ (k) $81^{-\frac{1}{2}}$ (l) $27^{-\frac{5}{3}}$

5 Write these numbers in full.

(a) 3.7×10^4 (b) 2.132×10^6 (c) 3.45×10^{-2} (d) 6×10^{-1}

6 Evaluate these expressions, leaving the answers in standard form.

(a) $9.4 \times 10^6 - 1\,234\,000$ (b) $\dfrac{3.5 \times 10^5}{7 \times 10^2}$ (c) $\dfrac{6.4 \times 10^3}{8 \times 10^{-5}}$

7 Write these numbers in standard form.

(a) 3500 (b) 2.84 (c) 15 400 (d) 498 000

(e) 7 million (f) 0.0476 (g) 5 billion (h) 5 750 200

8 Write these numbers in full.

(a) 6.3×10^4 (b) 5.8×10^{-2} (c) 9.223×10^4

(d) 5.64×10^5 (e) 6.4×10^{-3} (f) 6.24×10^7

9 Work out the following, leaving your answers in standard form.

(a) $4 \times 10^5 \times 2 \times 10^5$ (b) $8 \times 10^4 \div (4 \times 10^3)$

(c) $8 \times 10^{-2} \times 4 \times 10^6$ (d) $3 \times 10^3 \times 6 \times 10^6$

Unit 6
RATE, RATIO AND PROPORTION

Rate

If 12 kg of rice cost $18, how much do 8 kg cost? One way to find out is to work out the cost of 1 kg first.

$$12 \text{ kg cost} \quad \$18$$

$$1 \text{ kg costs} \quad \frac{\$18}{12}$$

$$8 \text{ kg cost} \quad \frac{\$18}{12} \times 8 = \$12$$

This is a **unitary method.** The cost of one unit is worked out first.

Example 1 My friend buys 3 kg of durians for $18.00. How much would 5 kg cost?

$$3 \text{ kg cost } \$18.00$$

$$1 \text{ kg costs } \frac{\$18}{3} = \$6$$

$$5 \text{ kg cost } \$6 \times 5 = \$30$$

Example 2 Telephone calls to Brazil cost B$0.60 per 6 seconds at the standard rate and B$0.53 per 6 seconds at the weekend rate. How much does a 3 minute phone call cost on weekdays and at the weekend?

On a weekday 6 seconds cost B$0.60
1 second costs B$0.60 ÷ 6 = B$0.10
3 minutes = 180 seconds cost B$0.10 × 180 = $18.00

At the weekend, the cost is B$$\frac{0.53}{6} \times 180 = $$ B$15.90

Speed, distance and time

The speed at which a car travels is usually measured in kilometres *per* hour, a distance divided by a time.

$$\text{Speed} = \frac{\text{Distance}}{\text{Time}}$$

This can also be written as **Distance = Speed × Time** and **Time** $= \dfrac{\text{Distance}}{\text{Speed}}$

Example A car left Bandar Seri Begawan at 4 p.m. and arrived in Tutong 60 km away in 45 minutes. What was the speed of the car in km/h? The distance = 60 km. The time is 45 minutes = $\frac{3}{4}$ hr. (The answer is required in km/h so the units have to be changed.)

$$S = \frac{D}{T} = \frac{60}{\frac{3}{4}} \text{ km/h} = 60 \div \frac{3}{4} \text{ km/h} = 60 \times \frac{4}{3} = 80 \text{ km/h}$$

Ratios

If two quantities are in the ratio 3 : 4 (we say '3 to 4'), then the first quantity is $\frac{3}{4}$ of the second quantity. We can use fractions to simplify ratios, for example, $8 : 4 = \frac{8}{4} = \frac{2}{1} = 2 : 1$

Ratios are sometimes written in the form $1 : a$ or $a : 1$.
For example, $20 : 16 = \frac{20}{16} = \frac{5}{4} = \frac{1.25}{1} = 1.25 : 1$.
If $a : b = 5 : 6$ and $b : c = 6 : 7$ then $a : b : c = 5 : 6 : 7$.

> A ratio statement such as $a : b = 5 : 6$ can be written in several other ways:
> $$\frac{a}{b} = \frac{5}{6} \quad \text{or } 6a = 5b \quad \text{or } \frac{a}{5} = \frac{b}{6} \quad \text{or } a = \frac{5}{6} b$$

Express quantities you are comparing in the same units.

Example 1 Express the ratio of 5 km to 300 m in its simplest form.

$$5 \text{ km} : 300 \text{ m} = \frac{5 \text{ km}}{300 \text{ m}} = \frac{5000 \text{ m}}{300 \text{ m}} = \frac{50}{3} = 50 : 3$$

In more difficult problems, three quantities are compared.

Example 2 If $a : b = 5 : 6$ and $b : c = 9 : 11$, what is $a : c$?

$$\frac{a}{b} = \frac{5}{6} \text{ and } \frac{b}{c} = \frac{9}{11} \text{ so } \frac{a}{b} \times \frac{b}{c} = \frac{a}{c} = \frac{5}{6} \times \frac{9}{11} = \frac{15}{22}. \text{ So } a : c = 15 : 22$$

Sharing in a given ratio

A man gives his two sons $10. The elder gets $6 and the younger $4. They share the $10 **in the ratio 6 : 4.** The elder gets $\frac{6}{10}$ of the money and the younger gets $\frac{4}{10}$ of the money. Note that the denominator 10 = 4 + 6.

Suppose the two boys share $40 in the ratio 5 : 3. How much does each get?
5 + 3 = 8, so they get $\frac{5}{8}$ of $40 and $\frac{3}{8}$ of $40 respectively.
$\frac{5}{8}$ of $40 = $25 and $\frac{3}{8}$ of $40 = $15.

> **If two people share a quantity in the ratio $a : b$, the first gets**
> $\dfrac{a}{a+b}$ **and the second gets** $\dfrac{b}{a+b}$ **of the total quantity.**

Example   A stick 20 cm long is divided into 3 pieces in the ratio 2 : 3 : 5. How long is each piece?
5 + 3 + 2 = 10, so the pieces are $\frac{5}{10}$, $\frac{3}{10}$ and $\frac{2}{10}$ of the total length.
$\frac{5}{10}$ of 20 cm = 10 cm; $\frac{3}{10}$ of 20 cm = 6 cm, and $\frac{2}{10}$ of 20 cm = 4 cm.

Increasing and decreasing in a given ratio

The number in a class increases from 25 to 30.
The number has increased in the ratio 30 : 25. (The larger number is stated first.)

If the number decreased from 25 to 20, then the number has decreased in the ratio 20 : 25. (The smaller number is first.)

> **If a quantity is increased/decreased in the ratio $a : b$,**
> **then the new quantity is** $\dfrac{a}{b} \times$ **old quantity.**
>
> **For an increase,** $\dfrac{a}{b} > 1$. **For a decrease,** $\dfrac{a}{b} < 1$.

Example 1   The price of a radio was $120. If the price is increased in the ratio 6 : 5, what is the new price?
   The new price is $120 \times \dfrac{6}{5} = 144

Example 2   The price of a suit is $150. If prices in a sale are reduced in the ratio 3 : 5, what is the sale price of the suit?
   The sale price is $150 \times \dfrac{3}{5} = 90

Direct proportion

If one bag of rice costs $3, then 2 bags cost 2 × $3 = $6. The more rice is bought, the more it costs. If one man can dig 3 holes in one hour, then 2 men can dig 2 × 3 = 6 holes on one hour. The more men, the more holes they can dig in an hour. These are examples of **direct proportion**.

Example 1   If 7 CDs cost $56, how much will 5 CDs cost?

Here are two ways of doing it.

(i) Unitary method:

7 CDs cost $56

1 CD costs $\dfrac{\$56}{7}$

5 CDs cost $5 \times \dfrac{\$56}{7} = \$40$

(ii) Proportional method:

7 CDs cost $56

5 CDs cost $\$56 \times \dfrac{5}{7} = \$40$

Example 2   8 tailors can make 28 suits in a day. How many suits can 20 tailors make in a day?

20 tailors can make $28 \times \dfrac{20}{8}$ suits = 70 suits

Inverse proportion

A woman has $20 to buy rice. She can buy 10 packets if they cost $2 each, but only 5 packets if the rice costs $4. The more expensive the rice, the less she can buy with her money. The more workers there are doing a job, the less time they take to do it. Double the number of workers and the time for a job is halved. These are examples of quantities in **inverse** or **indirect** proportion. Two quantities are in inverse proportion if an increase (or decrease) in one causes a decrease (or increase) in the other.

Example   8 men can build a wall in 12 days. How long will 6 men take to build it?

(i)   Unitary method:

8 men take 12 days

So 1 man takes 12 × 8 days (one man takes longer, so multiply)

6 men take 12 × 8 ÷ 6 days = 16 days (6 men take less time, so divide)

(ii) Proportional method:

6 men take longer; the ratio of the time taken is 8 : 6

The time taken = $12 \times \dfrac{8}{6} = 16$ days

1 If 8 apples cost $1.80, how much do 12 apples cost?

2 If 3 kg of soap powder costs $18.00, how much does 2 kg cost?

3 Potatoes are sold in two sizes of bags. 2 kg bags cost $3.50 and 3 kg bags cost $4. Which size is the better bargain for the customer?

4 Telephone calls to Kuala Lumpur cost $0.21 per 6 seconds on weekdays and $0.15 for 6 seconds at the weekend. How much does it cost to ring Kuala Lumpur
   (a) for 5 minutes on Tuesday afternoon
   (b) for 6 minutes 18 seconds on Sunday afternoon?

5 A cake recipe to serve 4 people requires:
   300 g butter   400 g sugar   600 g flour   200 g currants
   (a) How much flour is needed to make a cake for 8 people?
   (b) How much butter is needed to make a cake for 6 people?
   (c) If 1 kg of sugar is used to make a cake, how much flour is needed?

6 A boy cycles at 24 km/h for 2 hours 25 minutes. How far does he travel?

7 A car leaves Bandar Seri Begawan for Kuala Belait at 9 a.m. travelling at 80 km/h. At the same time, a car leaves Kuala Belait for Bandar Seri Begawan travelling at 60 km/h. The distance from Bandar Seri Begawan to Kuala Belait is 105 km. At what time do the two cars meet?

8 Simplify (a) 21 : 15   (b) 2.5 : 7.5

9 Simplify (a) 5 cm : 2 m   (b) 3 hours : 45 min   (c) 2 kg : 250 g

10 Divide (a) $650 in the ratio 3 : 4 : 6   (b) $4 in the ratio 1 : 2 : 5   (c) 1 m in the ratio 5 : 7 : 8

11 Two brothers share $60 in the ratio 7 : 3. What is the difference between the amounts that they receive?

12 Three people share $63 000 in the ratio 2 : 3 : 4. How much is the smallest share?

13 An alloy is composed of copper, zinc and tin in the ratio 2 : 3 : 5. How much copper is there in 1 tonne of the alloy?

14 Two brothers share $100 in the ratio 2 : x. If one brother receives $60, calculate x.

15 The ratio of boys to girls in a school is 3 : 5. There are 450 boys. How many girls are there? What percentage of the pupils are boys?

16 A bag contains sweets. When they are divided equally amongst 12 children, each one gets 9 sweets. How many will each get if they are shared by 18 children?

Unit 7
MEASURES

Lengths and perimeters

In the metric system, the important measures of lengths are the millimetre, centimetre, metre and kilometre.

Name	Short form		Used for
Millimetre	mm	10 mm = 1 cm	Very short distances: floppy discs are 1 mm thick
Centimetre	cm	100 cm = 1 m	Short distances: a CD is about 10 cm across
Metre	m		Medium distances: most doors are 2 m tall
Kilometre	km	1000 m = 1 km	Long distances: BSB to KB is 100 km

'Milli' means a thousandth, 'centi' means a hundredth, and 'kilo' means a thousand.

When a problem has lengths in different units, it is usually sensible to change all the units so that they are the same.

Example What percentage is 25 cm of 5 m?

5 m = 500 cm so the answer is $\frac{25}{500} \times 100\% = 5\%$

Measuring a line in mm and cm

You may be asked to measure the length of lines in cm or mm. To measure the length of a straight line, put a ruler next to the line. Make sure that one end of the line is next to the 0 mark on the ruler, and look at the other end of the line. Read off the distance.

Point A is on the 0 mark. B is between the 2.5 and 2.6 cm marks. It is nearer to 2.5 cm.
AB = 2.5 cm or 25 mm.

D is between the 3.9 and 4.0 cm marks. It is nearer to 4.0 cm.
CD = 4.0 cm or 40 mm.

Perimeter

The perimeter of shape is the distance all the way round it.
It is worked out by adding up the lengths of all the sides.
For example, the perimeter of this triangle is 3 + 5 + 6 cm = 14 cm.

This rectangle has a perimeter of 4 + 6 + 4 + 6 cm = 20 cm.

There is a formula for the perimeter of a rectangle:

P, the perimeter $= l + b + l + b$
$= 2l + 2b$
$= 2(l + b)$

In the example above, $l = 6$ cm and $b = 4$ cm,
so $P = 2(6 + 4) = 2 \times 10 = 20$ cm, so the perimeter is 20 cm. It is not necessary to remember this formula. It is easier to add up the lengths of the sides.

Circumference and length of arc of a circle

The diagram shows a circle.
The **circumference** is the curved line whose points
are all the same distance from the centre, O, of the circle.
This distance is the **radius**, r, of the circle.

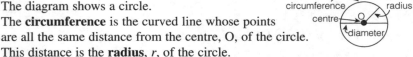

Any straight line from the centre to the circumference is called a radius.
Any straight line across the circle through the centre is a **diameter**. The diameter, d, of a circle is the length of any of these diameters.
The diameter is twice the radius: $d = 2r$
By measuring, it can be shown that the length of the circumference $C = \pi d = 2\pi r$ where π is 3.14159... π is approximately $\frac{22}{7}$ or 3.14
Press the π button on your calculator for a more accurate value of π. It is an irrational number and the decimal expansion goes on for ever.
A semicircle has a curved length of half of the circle $= \frac{1}{2} \times 2\pi r = \pi r$

    The length of arc is $\dfrac{A}{360} \times 2\pi r$

Example 1   A slice of a cake is a 50° sector of a circle radius 12 cm.
What is the perimeter of this slice? (Give the answer to 3 s.f.)

    Curved length is $\dfrac{A}{360} \times 2\pi r = \dfrac{5}{360} \times 2 \times 3.14 \times 12$ cm
$= 10.5$ cm

The perimeter = 10.5 + 12 + 12 cm = 34.5 cm

39

> **Perimeter of a polygon is the sum of the lengths of its sides.**
> **Circumference of a circle, $C = \pi d = 2\pi r$**
> **Length of arc with sector angle $A°$ of circle radius r is $\dfrac{A}{360} \times 2\pi r$**

Perimeter problems often involve composite figures.

Example 2 In the figure, three semicircles are on a 4 cm square. What is the perimeter of the figure? (Take π to be 3.14.)

The perimeter is one side of the square + 3 semicircles

$= 4 + 3 \times \frac{1}{2} \times 2\pi r = 4 + 3 \times 0.5 \times 2 \times 3.14 \times 2 = 22.84$ cm

4 cm

Mass and density

The **mass** of an object is measured in grams (g), kilograms (kg) and tonnes (t).

Name	Short form		Used for
Gram	g	1000 g = 1 kg	Small masses: a pencil is about 5 g
Kilogram	kg	1000 cm = 1 t	Medium masses: most adults are 70–80 kg
Tonne	t		Large masses: a car is about 1 t

Example 1 Convert 4352 g to kilograms.

4352 g = $\frac{4352}{1000}$ kg = 4.352 kg

The **density** of a substance, in g/cm^3, is the mass of 1 cm^3 of the substance.
Density of a substance = Mass/Volume
or   **Mass = Density × Volume**
or   **Volume = Mass/Density**

Example 2 What is the density in g/cm^3 of a substance if 5 m^3 of the substance weighs 3 tonnes?

$\text{Density} = \dfrac{\text{Mass}}{\text{Volume}} = \dfrac{3 \text{ tonnes}}{5 \text{ m}^3}$

$= \dfrac{3 \times 1000 \times 1000 \text{ gm}}{5 \times 100 \times 100 \times 100 \text{ cm}^3} = \dfrac{3}{5} \text{ gm/cm}^3 = 0.6 \text{ gm/cm}^3$

Example 3 What is the mass of 2 cm of rain falling on a roof that is a 20 m by 6 m rectangle? (The density of water is 1 gm/cm^3.)

Mass = Density × Volume

$= 1 \text{ gm/cm}^3 \times 2 \text{ cm} \times 20 \text{ m} \times 6 \text{ m}$

$= 1 \text{ gm/cm}^3 \times 2 \text{ cm} \times 2000 \text{ cm} \times 600 \text{ cm}$

$= \dfrac{1 \times 2 \times 2000 \times 600}{1000 \times 1000} \text{ t} = \dfrac{24}{10} \text{ t} = 2.4 \text{ tonnes}$

Time

The measurement of time does not follow the metric system. A day is the time that it takes for the Earth to rotate once. A day is divided into hours, minutes and seconds.

> **60 seconds (s) = 1 minute (min)**
> **60 minutes = 1 hour (h)**
> **24 hours (h) = 1 day**

Example   Change   (a) 8 h 40 min into seconds   (b) 8040 s into hours and minutes

(a) 8 h 40 min = 8 × 60 + 40 minutes = 520 minutes
     520 minutes = 520 × 60 seconds = 31 200 seconds
(b) 8040 s = 8040 ÷ 60 min = 134 min = 2 h 14 min

Time and decimals

Time problems often have answers with decimals in them. These can be converted into hours and minutes.

Example   How long will it take to travel 110 km at a speed of 80 km/h?

$$T = \frac{D}{S} = \frac{110}{80} = 1.375 \text{ h}$$

0.375 h is not 37.5 min.
0.375 h = 0.375 × 60 minutes = 22.5 min = 22 min 30 s
This can also be done on a calculator:
Type in 1.375 and then press the degrees button to read 1°22°30 or 1°22′30′ (depending on the calculator) which means 1 h 22 min 30 sec.

Longer periods of time are measured in years, months and weeks.

Week	**= 7 days**
Month	**Time for Moon to go around Earth (approximately)**
Year	**Time for Earth to go around Sun**
1 year	**= 365 days (366 in leap year)**
	= 52 weeks + 1 day (52 weeks + 2 days in leap year)
	= 12 months

There are two ways of telling the time of day.

12-hour clock
On a 12-hour clock, the day is divided into two twelve-hour periods. The day starts at midnight. The period from midnight to noon is 'a.m.' which is short

for 'ante meridiem' meaning 'before mid-day'. The period from noon to mid-night is 'p.m.', short for 'post meridiem' meaning 'after mid-day'.

Asleep	School starts	School finishes	Evening
12.00 midnight	7.30 a.m.	12.30 p.m.	7.30 p.m.

The 12-hour clock is the time that is used in everyday life and on watches.

Example   How long is the time between (a) 4.15 a.m. and 9.42 p.m.
(b) 6.42 p.m. and 8.30 a.m. the following day?

(a) 4.15 a.m. to 12 noon is   7 h 45 min   [45 + 42 min = 87 min
    12 noon to 9.42 p.m. is   <u>9 h 42 min</u>   = 1 h 27 min, so the 1 h is
                           17 h 27 min   carried into the hours column]

(b) 6.42 p.m. to midnight is   5 h 18 min
    12 midnight to 8.30 a.m. is <u>8 h 30 min</u>
                           13 h 48 min

24-hour clock

The 24-hour clock is used for airline timetables. The day is one 24-hour period. Times between midnight and noon go from 0000 to 1200 hours. Times from noon to midnight go from 1200 to 2400 hours.

Asleep	School starts	School finishes	Evening
0000	0730	1230	1930

The 12-hour clock time of 5.45 a.m. is written 0545 (and read as 'five forty-five hours').
5.45 p.m. is written 1745 (and read as 'seventeen forty-five hours').
The time of 1600 is read as 'sixteen hundred hours'.

Example   How long is the time between (a) 0543 and 1922 (b) 1642 and 0927 the following day?

Separate the hours and minutes in these problems.

(a) 1922 is   19̸ h 22 min
    0543 is   − <u>5 h 43 min</u>
                              13 h 39 min

[22 min − 43 min cannot be done so 1 hour = 60 minutes is added to the minutes column.]

(b) Midnight is   24̸ h 00 min
    1642 is   − <u>16 h 42 min</u>
                             7 h 18 min
    Midnight to 0927   <u>9 h 27 min</u>
                              16 h 45 min

Temperature

Some important temperatures measured in **degrees Celsius** are:
The boiling point of water at sea level: 100°C
The freezing point of water at sea level: 0°C
The normal temperature of our blood: 37.4°C

MEASURES – TYPICAL QUESTIONS

1 Measure the lengths of these lines.
(a) ——————————————————————
(b) ————————————————————
(c) ——————————————

2 Convert these lengths to metres.
(a) 4.5 km   (b) 2 km 850 m   (c) 650 cm

3 Find the perimeter of a 10 cm by 6 cm rectangle.

4 What is the circumference of each of these circles?
(a) radius 20 cm (let $\pi = 3.14$)   (b) diameter 50 cm (let $\pi = 3.14$)
(c) radius 28 cm (let $\pi = \frac{22}{7}$)   (d) diameter 0.7 cm (let $\pi = \frac{22}{7}$)

5 Find the diameter of these circles.
(a) circumference 6280 km (let $\pi = 3.14$)
(b) circumference 44 m (let $\pi = \frac{22}{7}$)

6 Find the length of a 70° arc of a circle with a radius of 9 cm (let $\pi = \frac{22}{7}$).

7 What is the density of a solid with a mass of 1 kg and a volume of 80 cm³ ?

8 Convert   (a) 834 g to kg   (b) 12 kg to g   (c) 2.5 kg to g
(d) 5800 mg to g   (e) 5.8 kg to g   (f) 4560 kg to t

9 Express   (a) 350 g as a percentage of 2 kg
(b) 50 m as a percentage of 1 km
(c) 48 min as a fraction of 3 hours

10 A plane left Singapore for Bandar Seri Begawan at 12.35 p.m. The flight took 1 hour and 45 minutes. At what time did the aircraft reach Bandar Seri Begawan?

11 A man left home at 14.25. He reached Tutong at 15.50. How long was his journey?

12 A rectangle is 60 cm long and 40 cm wide.
(a) What is its perimeter?
(b) Its length is increased by 20%. What is its new length?
(c) Its breadth is increased by 10%. What is its new breadth?
(d) What is its new perimeter?
(e) What is the percentage increase in perimeter?

Unit 8
AREA

Area of rectangles

The 5 cm by 3 cm rectangle in the diagram is divided into 1 cm squares. There are 15 squares. The **area** of the rectangle is 15 square centimetres = 5×3 square centimetres (15 cm^2).

A rectangle 4 cm by 6 cm can be divided into 24 one-cm squares. It has an area of 4×6 cm^2 = 24 cm^2.

The **area of a rectangle is length × breadth**.
If length = l cm, breadth = b cm, area in cm^2,
$A = l \times b$
The area of a square is **length × length**.
If the length of a side is s cm, the area in cm^2,
$A = s^2$

Example   A rectangle has a length of 24 m and a breadth of 20 m. The length is increased by 25% and the breadth by 20%.

(a) What is the area of the original rectangle?
(b) What are the length and breadth of the new, larger rectangle?
(c) What is the area of the new, larger rectangle?
(d) What is the percentage increase in area?

(a) Area = length × breadth
    = 24 m × 20 m = 480 m^2

(b) The length has increased by 25% to 125% of its old length.
    New length = 125% of 24 m = 1.25 × 24 m = 30 m
    New breadth = 120% of 20 m = 1.20 × 20 m = 24 m

(c) New area = length × breadth = 30 × 24 m = 720 m^2

(d) Increase in area = 720 − 480 m^2 = 240 m^2
    % increase = $\dfrac{240}{480} \times 100\%$ = 50%

Units of area

Areas are stated in square millimetres (mm²), square centimetres (cm²), square metres (m²), square kilometres (km²) or hectares.

A hectare is the area of a 100 m square.

> **1 hectare = 100 m × 100 m = 10 000 m²**
> **1 km² = 1000 m × 1000 m = 1 000 000 m² = 10⁶ m²**
> **1 m² = 100 cm × 100 cm = 10 000 cm² = 10⁴ cm²**
> **1 cm² = 10 mm × 10 mm = 100 mm² = 10² mm²**

Example   How many 20 cm by 20 cm tiles are needed to cover a floor measuring 5 m by 6 m?

Area of a tile = 20 cm × 20 cm

Area of floor = 5 m × 6 m = 500 cm × 600 cm

Number of tiles = $\frac{500 \times 600}{20 \times 20}$ = 25 × 30 = 750

(Make sure that the units are the same for the area of the tiles and the floor.)

Area of triangles

All triangles have a base and a height for that base.

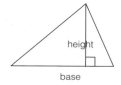 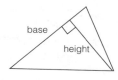

All triangles are half a rectangle and have an area of half the rectangle containing them.

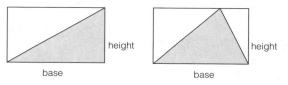

> **Area of triangle = ½ base × height**

Example   In this rectangle AB = 6 cm and BC = 4 cm. The diagonals meet at O.

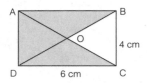

(a) Find the area of triangles AOB and BOC.
(b) Find the area of the shaded part.

(a) Area of triangle AOB = $\frac{1}{2}$ base × height = $\frac{1}{2}$ × 6 × 2 cm^2 = 6 cm^2
Area of triangle BOC = $\frac{1}{2}$ × 4 × 3 cm^2 = 6 cm^2

(b) Shaded area = area of rectangle – area triangle BOC
$$= 4 \times 6 - 6 \text{ cm}^2 = 24 - 6 \text{ cm}^2 = 18 \text{ cm}^2$$

Area of parallelograms and trapezia

A **parallelogram** has two pairs of opposite sides parallel to each other. If one side is the base, the distance between that side and the side parallel to it is the **height**.

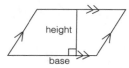   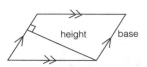

A parallelogram can be divided into two triangles.

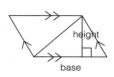

Each triangle has an area of $\frac{1}{2}$ base × height of the parallelogram.
Area of parallelogram = 2 × area of triangle
$$= 2 \times \tfrac{1}{2} \text{ base} \times \text{height}$$
$$= \textbf{base} \times \textbf{height}$$

A **trapezium** has a pair of opposite sides parallel. In the diagram, the trapezium has parallel sides of lengths a and b and they area distance h apart.

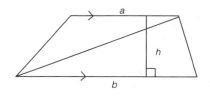

Divide the trapezium into two triangles.
Both have a height of h.
They have areas of $\frac{1}{2}ah$ and $\frac{1}{2}bh$.
Area of trapezium = $\frac{1}{2}ah + \frac{1}{2}bh$
$$= \tfrac{1}{2}(a + b)\, h$$

46

Example   Find the area of

(a) triangle ABC and

(b) trapezium ABCD in this diagram.

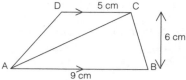

(a) Area of triangle ABC = $\frac{1}{2}$ base × height

                     = $\frac{1}{2}$ × 9 × 6 cm^2 = 27 cm^2

(b) Area of trapezium ABCD = $\frac{1}{2}$ (a + b) h

                            = $\frac{1}{2}$ (5 + 9) × 6 cm^2 = $\frac{1}{2}$ × 14 × 6 cm^2 = 42 cm^2

Area of circles and sectors of circles

The area of a circle radius r is πr^2.

A semicircle has an area of half of the circle = $\frac{1}{2}$ × πr^2.

semicircle

The area of a quarter circle is $\frac{1}{4}$ × πr^2.

quarter circle

Area of shaded sector is $\dfrac{a}{360}$ × πr^2.

[This formula is usually stated on the examination paper.]

Example   A circle has a radius of 15 cm. What is the area of a sector of the circle with an angle of 80°?

Area = $\dfrac{a}{360}$ × πr^2 cm^2 = $\dfrac{80}{360}$ × 3.14 × 15 × 15 cm^2 = 157 cm^2

> **Area of rectangle = length × breadth = $l\,b$**
>
> **Area of square = side × side = s^2**
>
> **Area of triangle = $\frac{1}{2}$ base × height = $\frac{1}{2}\,bh$**
>
> **Area of parallelogram = base × height = bh**
>
> **Area of trapezium = $\frac{1}{2}$ (a + b) h**
>
> **Area of circle = πr^2**
>
> **Area of sector = $\dfrac{\text{Angle}}{360}\,\pi r^2$**

AREA – TYPICAL QUESTIONS

1 Find the area of each of these figures.

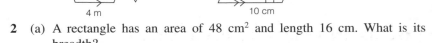

(a) 5 m, 8 m

(b) 7 cm, 6 cm

(c) 6 m, 5 m, 4 m

(d) 12 cm, 10 cm

2 (a) A rectangle has an area of 48 cm² and length 16 cm. What is its breadth?

(b) A triangle has an area of 66 cm² and a height of 11 cm. How long is its base?

(c) A trapezium has parallel sides of 6 cm and 8 cm and an area of 84 cm². How far apart are the parallel sides?

(d) A parallelogram has sides all 8 cm long and an area of 40 cm². How far apart are the sides?

3 (a) Two circles have areas in the ratio 16 : 49. What is the ratio of their diameters?

(b) Two squares have sides in the ratio 5 : 3. What is the ratio of their areas?

(c) The ratio of the radii of the two circles A and B is 4 : 5. The area of circle A is 80 cm². What is the area of circle B?

4 A round mirror has radius 10 cm. It is inside a circular frame radius 30 cm. What is the area of the frame? Take π = 3.14 and give your answer to 3 s.f.

5 A rectangular picture measures 30 cm by 20 cm. It is surrounded by a frame that is 2 cm wide. What is the area of the frame?

6 How many tiles 20 cm by 10 cm are needed to tile a floor 5 m by 4 m?

Unit 9 _____
SURFACE AREA AND VOLUME

Solids and their nets

Many objects have common geometric names.
Play blocks are usually **cubes.** Bricks are **cuboids.**
Balls are often **spheres** (although footballs are not).
Milo tins are **cylinders.** Ice creams are sold in **cones.**

Solids have **faces, edges** and **vertices**.
The **surface area** of a solid is the sum of the areas of all its faces.
The **volume** of a solid is the amount of space it occupies.

Cubes

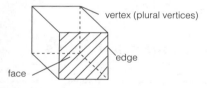

All 6 **faces** are squares that are the same size.
All 12 **edges** are the same length.
Angles between faces at the
8 **vertices** are all 90°.

The **net** of a cube is what you get when you fold the cube out. The number of shapes in the net is the number of faces of the cube.
When making a net, put flaps on it to make it easy to stick together.
The surface area of a solid is the same as the area of its net (without the flaps).

Cuboids

All 6 **faces** are rectangles. Opposite rectangles are identical.
There are 12 **edges**, in three sets of 4 congruent rectangles.
Angles between faces at the 8 **vertices** are all 90°.

Pyramids

A pyramid has a flat base and edges rising to a point. The sloping edges are all triangles. The shape of the base is included in the name.

Triangular-based pyramid (tetrahedron)	Square-based pyramid	Hexagonal-based pyramid
	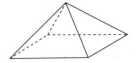	
4 faces, 4 vertices, 6 edges	5 faces, 5 vertices, 8 edges	7 faces, 7 vertices, 12 edges

A cone is a pyramid with a circular base.

Pyramids and **cones** all have volumes that are $\frac{1}{3}$ **area of the base × height**.

Prisms

The cube, cuboid and cylinder are all examples of **prisms**. A prism is like a loaf of bread – when you cut it, all the pieces are the same shape.
The volume of any prism = **area of its base × its height**.

Surface areas and volumes of important solids

Solid	Net	Total surface area	Volume
Cube		Base = $l \times l$ Total surface area $= 6l^2$	Vol. = Area of the base × height $= l \times l \times l$ $= l^3$
Cuboid		Total surface area $= 2\,lb + 2\,lh + 2\,bh$ $= 2(lb + lh + bh)$	Vol. = Area of the base × height $= l \times b \times h$
Cylinder		Total surface area $= (2\pi r \times h) + (\pi r^2 + \pi r^2)$ $= 2\pi rh + 2\pi r^2$ $= 2\pi r(h + r)$	Vol. = Area of the base × height $= \pi r^2\, h$

Solid	Net	Total surface area	Volume
Square-based pyramid		Total surface area $= 4(\frac{1}{2}\,ah) + a^2$ $= 2\,ah + a^2$	Vol. $= \frac{1}{3} \times$ Area of the base $\times$ height $= \frac{1}{3}\,a^2 \times h$ ($\frac{1}{3}$ volume of a cuboid with the same height and base)
Cone		Area of the curved surface $= \frac{2\pi r}{2\pi l} \times \pi l^2$ $= \pi\,r\,l$ Area of the base $= \pi r^2$ Total surface area $= \pi r l + \pi r^2 = \pi r(l + r)$	Vol. $= \frac{1}{3}\pi r^2 h$ ($\frac{1}{3}$ volume of a cylinder with the same height and base)
Sphere		Total surface area $= 4\pi r^2$	Vol. $= \frac{4}{3}\,\pi r^3$

Example 1

The radius of a sphere is 42 cm. Find the surface area and volume of the sphere. (Take $\pi = \frac{22}{7}$)

Surface area of the sphere is $4\pi r^2 = 4 \times \frac{22}{7} \times 42 \times 42$ cm^2 = 22 176 cm^2

Volume of the sphere is $\frac{4}{3}\pi r^3 = \frac{4}{3} \times \frac{22}{7} \times 42 \times 42 \times 42$ cm^3 = 310 464 cm^3

Example 2

The area of the base of a triangular prism is 50 cm^2. The height of the prism is 4 cm. Find its volume.

Volume of the prism = area of base $\times$ height
$$= 50 \text{ cm}^2 \times 4 \text{ cm} = 200 \text{ cm}^3$$

Example 3

The diagram shows a pyramid on a rectangular base ABCD. AB = 32 cm, BC = 18 cm and the vertical line EF = 12 cm. FG = 15 cm and FH = 20 cm. Calculate (a) its total surface area (b) its volume.

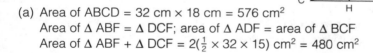

(a) Area of ABCD = 32 cm $\times$ 18 cm = 576 cm^2
Area of $\triangle$ ABF = $\triangle$ DCF; area of $\triangle$ ADF = area of $\triangle$ BCF
Area of $\triangle$ ABF + $\triangle$ DCF = $2(\frac{1}{2} \times 32 \times 15)$ cm^2 = 480 cm^2

Area of $\triangle$ ADF + $\triangle$ BCF = $2(\frac{1}{2} \times 18 \times 20)$ cm^2 = 360 cm^2

Total surface area of the pyramid = 576 + 480 + 360 cm^2 = 1416 cm^2

(b) Volume of the pyramid = $\frac{1}{3}$ volume of the cuboid with base ABCD

   = $\frac{1}{3} \times 32$ cm $\times 18$ cm $\times 12$ cm = 2304 cm^3

SURFACE AREA AND VOLUME – TYPICAL QUESTIONS

1 The diagram shows the net of a square-based pyramid.
BC = 3 cm, AB = 4 cm. Find the total surface area
of the pyramid.

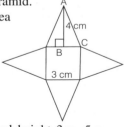

2 A closed rectangular tank with length, width and height 3 m, 5 m and
10 m respectively is $\frac{3}{4}$ full of water. Find
   (a) the total volume of the tank   (b) the total surface area of the tank
   (c) the amount of water in the tank.

3 In this question, take π to be 3.14. A solid cone has a base with a radius of
10 cm and a height of 12 cm. Calculate
   (a) the area of the base of the cone
   (b) the volume of the cone.
   Give your answers to 3 significant figures.

4 In the diagram, VABCD is a rectangular pyramid.
AB = 8 cm and BC = 6 cm.
The altitude VO = 10 cm.
Find the volume of the pyramid.

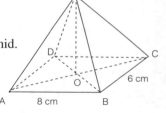

5 A cone has a height of 12 cm, a base radius of 5 cm and a slant height of
13 cm.
Assuming that π = 3.14, calculate
   (a) the volume of the cone
   (b) the surface area of the cone.

6 In this question, take π to be 3.14. Calculate the surface area and volume of
   (a) a sphere with a radius of 3 cm
   (b) a cone with a height and base radius of 10 cm and slant height of
       14.1 cm
   (c) a cuboid with a square base of side 10 cm and a height of 20 cm
   (d) a cylinder with a length of 2 cm and a base radius of 0.5 cm.
   Give your answers to 3 significant figures.

52

Unit 10
INTRODUCTION TO ALGEBRA

Representation of unknowns by symbols

The area of a rectangle = length × breadth. This is usually written more briefly as $A = l \times b$. The letters A, l and b are used as a short way of writing the numerical area, length and breadth of a rectangle.

$A = l \times b$ is an example of a formula (plural formulae or formulas). It states the relationship between A, l and b. The letters stand for numbers, not for area, length and breadth.

Letters are operated on by the same operations as numbers: addition, subtraction, multiplication and division.

2 more than 3 is 3 + 2 = 5	**2 more than x is $x + 2$**
The sum of 2 and 3 is 2 + 3	**The sum of x and y is $x + y$**
5 less than 8 is 8 – 5	**5 less than y is $y - 5$**
The difference between 8 and 5 is 8 – 5	**The difference between x and y if $x > y$ is $x - y$**

7 times 8 is 7 × 8, which is 56	**7 times m is $7 \times m$, which is written more briefly as $7m$.** **The × sign is left out. $8p$ means $8 \times p$.**
12 divided by 3 is 12 ÷ 3, which can be written as $= \frac{12}{3}$ or $^{12}/_3 = 4$	**12 divided by d is $12 \div d$, which can be written as $\frac{12}{d}$ or $^{12}/_d$**
	$2x + 3y$ means $2 \times x + 3 \times y$
3^2 means 3×3	**x^2 means $x \times x$ $p^5 = p \times p \times p \times p \times p$**

Be careful with letters and what they mean.
abc means $a \times b \times c$
ab^2 means $a \times b \times b$ not $(ab)^2$
$(ab)^2$ means $(ab) \times (ab) = a \times b \times a \times b = a \times a \times b \times b = a^2b^2$
$a(b - c)^2$ means $a(b - c)(b - c)$. Only the $(b - c)$ is squared.

A **term** is a group of numbers, letters and brackets that are multiplied together. Terms are separated from each other by + and − signs.

An **expression** is a collection of terms, such as $5x − 8x + 14y$.

Like terms have the same letters in them. $5x$ and $8x$ are like terms. $14y$ and $14y^2$ are unlike terms.

Simplifying expressions

The expression $5x − 8 + 4y + 7x − 3y + 2$ can be simplified. Put a ring around each term and the sign in front of it:

$\boxed{5x} \quad \boxed{-8} \quad \boxed{+4y} \quad \boxed{+7x} \quad \boxed{-3y} \quad \boxed{+2}$

(The first term often does not have a sign in front of it.)

Rewrite with the like terms together:

x terms y terms   number terms

$\boxed{5x} \;\; \boxed{+7x} \quad \boxed{+4y} \;\; \boxed{-3y} \quad \boxed{-8} \;\; \boxed{+2}$

$= 12x + y − 6$

Example   Simplify these expressions where possible:

(a) $5a + 3b − 2ab + 6b + 4ab + a^2$ (b) $6a − 7b + 3c$

(c) $-4x^2 + 6xy + 3y^2 − 2xy − x^2 − y^2$

(a) $\boxed{5a}\;\boxed{+3b}\;\boxed{-2ab}\;\boxed{+6b}\;\boxed{+4ab}\;\boxed{+a^2}$ = $5a \;\;\boxed{+3b}\;\boxed{+6b}\;\boxed{-2ab}\;\boxed{+4ab}\;\;+a^2$

$= 5a \;+\; 9b \;+\; 2ab \;+\; a^2$

(b) $6a − 7b + 3c$ cannot be simplified. It is already in its simplest form.

(c) $\boxed{-4x^2}\;\boxed{+6xy}\;\boxed{+3y^2}\;\boxed{-2xy}\;\boxed{-x^2}\;\boxed{-y^2}$ = $\boxed{-4x^2}\;\boxed{-x^2}\;\boxed{+6xy}\;\boxed{-2xy}\;\boxed{+3y^2}\;\boxed{-y^2}$

$= -5x^2 \;+\; 4xy \;+\; 2y^2$

Evaluating algebraic expressions

If $F = \frac{9}{5}(C + 32)$, the value of F for any value of C is worked out by replacing C by that number in the formula. This is called **substituting** in the formula.

For example, if $C = 8$, then $F = \frac{9}{5}(C + 32) = \frac{9}{5}(8 + 32) = \frac{9}{5}(40) = 72$

Example 1   If $A = \pi r^2 h$ and $\pi = 3.14$, find

(a) A if $r = 2$, $h = 25$ (b) r if $A = 6280$, $h = 5$.

(a) $A = \pi r^2 h = 3.14 \times 2^2 \times 25 = 3.14 \times 100 = 314$

(b) $6280 = 3.14\, r^2 \times 5$, so $r^2 = \dfrac{6280}{3.14 \times 5}$ and $r = \pm \sqrt{400} = \pm 20$

Example 2   If $v = \sqrt{u^2 + 2as}$, find

(a) v when $u = 20$, $a = 20$ and $s = 12.5$

(b) s when $v = 80$, $u = 60$ and $a = 10$.

54

(a) $v = \sqrt{u^2 + 2as} = \sqrt{20^2 + 2 \times 20 \times 12.5} = \sqrt{400 + 500} = \sqrt{900} = 30$

(b) $v = \sqrt{u^2 + 2as}$. Substituting, $80 = \sqrt{60^2 + 2 \times 10 \times s}$

Square to remove the square root sign: $80^2 = 60^2 + 2 \times 10 \times s$

So $s = \dfrac{80^2 - 60^2}{2 \times 10} = 140$

Linear equations

An equation is a statement with an equals sign in it. $5x - 17 = 23$ is a **linear** equation. (In linear equations the highest power of the unknown is 1.) Finding the value of x that makes this statement true is **solving** the equation. In the exam, you will be asked to solve equations.

One-operation equations

Example   Solve (a) $x + 5 = 12$ (b) $y - 8 = 17$ (c) $5x = 20$ (d) $\frac{x}{6} = 9$

(a) $x + 5 = 12$ What number plus 5 is 12? It is 7 since $7 + 5 = 12$.
Taking 5 from both sides of the equation, $x + 5 - 5 = 12 - 5$
$$x = 12 - 5 = 7$$

(b) $y - 8 = 17$ What number minus 8 leaves 17? It is 25 since $25 - 8 = 17$.
Adding 8 to both sides of the equation, $y - 8 + 8 = 17 + 8$
$$y = 17 + 8 = 25$$

(c) $5x = 20$ What number times 5 equals 20? It is 4 since $4 \times 5 = 20$.
Dividing both sides of the equation by 5, $\dfrac{5x}{5} = \dfrac{20}{5}$
$$x = 20 \div 5 = 4$$

(d) $\frac{x}{6} = 9$ What number divided by 6 is 9? It is 54 since $54 \div 6 = 9$.
Multiplying both sides of the equation by 6, $\frac{x}{6} \times 6 = 9 \times 6$
$$x = 9 \times 6 = 54$$

The operation on a term changes on the other side of the equation:
- Addition changes to Subtraction and Subtraction changes to Addition
- Multiplication changes to Division and Division changes to Multiplication.

Equations with more than one operation

Example 1   Solve $3x - 11 = 43$

There are two operations: $\times 3$ and $- 11$, so two steps are required.

Step 1   Add 11 to both sides: $3x - 11 + 11 = 43 + 11$
This moves 11 to the other side: $3x = 43 + 11 = 54$
The term in x is now on one side of the equals sign, the numerical term is on the other side.

Step 2   Divide both sides by 3: $\dfrac{3x}{3} = \dfrac{54}{3}$

$$x = 54 \div 3 = 18$$

Check to make sure you have not made a mistake.
If $x = 18$, $3x - 11 = 3 \times 18 - 11 = 54 - 11 = 43$, as in the question.
So the answer is correct.

Example 2   Solve $\frac{5}{4}x = 25$

Step 1   Multiply both sides by 4: $4 \times \dfrac{5}{4}x = 4 \times 25$ so $5x = 4 \times 25$

Step 2   Divide both sides by 5: $\dfrac{5x}{5} = \dfrac{4 \times 25}{5} = 4 \times 5 = 20$ so $x = 20$

These two steps can be done together.

Multiply both sides by $\frac{4}{5}$: $\dfrac{4}{5} \times \dfrac{5}{4}x = \dfrac{4}{5} \times 25$

$$x = \dfrac{4}{5} \times 25$$

$$= 20$$

Equations with letters on both sides

Collect all the letters together on one side of the equation, and all the numerical terms on the other side.

Example   Solve the equation: $7x - 8 = 3x + 12$

Subtract $3x$ from both sides: $7x - 8 - 3x = 3x + 12 - 3x$

$$7x - 8 - 3x = 12$$

$$4x - 8 = 12$$

Add 8 to both sides: $4x - 8 + 8 = 12 + 8$

$$4x = 20$$

Divide both sides by 4: $\dfrac{4x}{4} = \dfrac{20}{4}$ so $x = \frac{20}{4} = 5$

Equations with brackets

Example   Solve $5(x + 4) = 7(2x - 1)$

Remove the brackets first: $5x + 20 = 14x - 7$
Subtract $5x$ from both sides: $5x + 20 - 5x = 14x - 5x - 7$

$$20 = 9x - 7$$

This is the same as: $9x - 7 = 20$

$$9x = 27 \quad \text{so } x = 3$$

Equations with denominators

Example   Solve $\dfrac{3x + 1}{4} = \dfrac{4x - 8}{3}$

Remove the denominators first. Multiply both sides by the L.C.M. of 3 and 4, which is 12.

$$12\left(\dfrac{3x + 1}{4}\right) = 12\left(\dfrac{4x - 8}{3}\right)$$

Cancelling: $3(3x + 1) = 4(4x - 8)$

Multiplying out the brackets: $9x + 3 = 16x - 32$

Rearranging: $35 = 7x$ so $x = 5$

EXAM TIP ✔

Steps in solving linear equations
1. **Remove denominators.**
2. **Multiply out brackets.**
3. **Collect all the terms in the unknown on one side of the equation.**
4. **Combine like terms.**
5. **Divide** (so as to leave the letter on its own).

INTRODUCTION TO ALGEBRA – TYPICAL QUESTIONS

1 Write down an expression for the number that is
  (a) six more than x (b) 12 less than p (c) 8 times x squared
  (d) three-quarters of y (e) the sum of x and y (f) p times q all squared.

2 Express the following in their simplest form:
  (a) $5xy - 3x - 4y + 3xy - y + 4x$ (b) $4x + 7y - 3x - 2y$
  (c) $8x^2 + 6 + x - 2 - 4x^2 - 2x$ (d) $3m + 2n - m - 2n$
  (e) $8ab + 6bc + ca - 2ba - 4cb$

3 If $a = 3$, $b = -4$ and $c = -2$, evaluate
  (a) $3a + 4b$ (b) $2a^2 - c$ (c) $ab + bc + ca$
  (d) abc (e) $4a^2 - 3b^2$ (f) $a^3 - b^3$

In questions 4–7, solve the equations.

4 (a) $x + 5 = 2$ (b) $y - 5 = -7$ (c) $3x = -18$
  (d) $x \div 5 = -6$ (e) $\frac{3}{5}x = 15$ (f) $-\frac{22}{7}x = 66$

5 (a) $5x - 17 = 23$ (b) $3x + 20 = 11$ (c) $28 = 10 - 3x$
  (d) $3x - 4 = 2x + 1$ (e) $3x - 8 = 7x$ (f) $5x - 3 = 2x + 9$

6 (a) $5(x - 2) = 4(x - 1)$ (b) $4(x + 3) = 20$ (c) $2(x - 1) = 4x - 5$
  (d) $2(3x + 4) = 8x$ (e) $3(5 - 3x) = 24$ (f) $2(x - 2) = 4(4 - 2x)$

7 (a) $\dfrac{7x - 2}{5} = 8$ (b) $\dfrac{5x + 1}{2} = \dfrac{2x + 7}{3}$ (c) $\dfrac{x + 10}{2} = \dfrac{2 - 5x}{3}$

  (d) $\dfrac{5x - 7}{2} = 3(x - 2)$ (e) $\dfrac{2}{3x - 5} = \dfrac{6}{2x - 1}$ (f) $\dfrac{3x - 1}{2} = \dfrac{8x - 1}{5}$

Unit 11 _____

ALGEBRAIC EXPRESSIONS
AND FORMULAE

Expansion of brackets

A number or letter outside a bracket multiplies every term inside the bracket.
This can be illustrated with a rectangle.

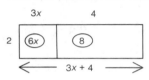

The total area of the large rectangle is $2(3x + 4)$
Area of the 2 small rectangles is $2 \times 3x + 2 \times 4$
The two areas are the same:
$2(3x + 4) = 2 \times 3x + 2 \times 4$
$\qquad\qquad = 6x + 8$
Similarly $2(3x - 4) = 2 \times 3x - 2 \times 4 = 6x - 8$

A negative sign reverses the signs in the bracket:
$$-2(3x - 4) = -2 \times 3x - (-2) \times 4 = -6x + 8$$

In letters:

$$a(b + c) = a \times b + a \times c$$
$$a(b - c) = a \times b - a \times c$$
$$(b + c)a = b \times a + c \times a$$

For example, $7x(x - y) = 7x^2 - 7xy$ $(x + 2y)xy^2 = x^2y^2 + 2xy^3$

To add brackets together, multiply them out and add like terms.

$$a + (b - c) = a + b - c$$
$$a + k(b + c) = a + kb + kc$$
$$a + k(b - c) = a + kb - kc$$

For example, $3(2x - y) + 4(3x + 2y) = 6x - 3y + 12x + 8y = 18x + 5y$

When a bracket is subtracted, the negative sign in front of the bracket changes
all the signs inside the bracket.

$$a - (b - c) = a - b + c$$
$$a - k(b - c) = a - kb + kc$$

For example, $3(x - 3) - (x - 5) = 3x - 9 - x + 5 = 2x - 4$
$\qquad\qquad\qquad 3(a - 2b) - 2(a + 3b) = 3a - 6b - 2a - 6b = a - 12b$

Multiplying out two brackets can also be illustrated by drawing a rectangle.

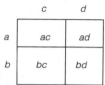

The area of the large rectangle is $(a + b)(c + d)$
This is the same as the sum of the areas of the small rectangles, $ac + ad + bc + bd$
So $(a + b)(c + d) = ac + ad + bc + bd$

Every term in a bracket is multiplied with every term in the other bracket. So we have

$$(a + b)(c + d) = a(c + d) + b(c + d) = ac + ad + bc + bd$$

$(x + a)(x + b) = x^2 + bx + ax + ab$
$\qquad\qquad\quad = x^2 + (a + b)x + ab$
$(x + a)^2 \quad\;\; = x^2 + ax + ax + ab$
$\qquad\qquad\quad = x^2 + 2ax + a^2$

$(x - a)(x - b) = x^2 - bx - ax + ab$
$\qquad\qquad\quad = x^2 - (a + b)x + ab$
$(ax + b)^2 \quad = a^2x^2 + abx + abx + b^2$
$\qquad\qquad\quad = a^2x^2 + 2abx + b^2$

For example,
$(x + 5)(x - 2) \quad = x^2 - 2x + 5x - 10 = x^2 + 3x - 10$
$(3y - 1)(4y + 3) = 12y^2 + 9y - 4y - 3 = 12y^2 + 5y - 3$
$(4x + 3y)(3x - y) = 12x^2 - 4xy + 9xy - 3y^2 = 12x^2 + 5xy - 3y^2$
$(x + 3)^2 \qquad\quad = x^2 + 2 \times x \times 3 + 3^2 = x^2 + 6x + 9$
$(4x - 3)^2 \qquad\quad = 16x^2 - 24x + 9$

The last two examples are examples of a **perfect square.**
The sum of two terms multiplied by their difference is known as the **difference of two squares**:

$$(a + b)(a - b) = a^2 - ab + ab - b^2 = a^2 - b^2$$

For example, $\quad (3x - 2y)(3x + 2y) = (3x)^2 - (2y)^2 = 9x^2 - 4y^2$

Factorisation by finding common factors and by grouping

Two terms

$5 \times 7 = 35 \qquad$ 5 and 7 are **factors** of 35.
$2(x - 4) = 2x - 8 \quad$ 2 and $(x - 4)$ are factors of $2x - 8$.

When factorising an expression, look for the common factors of all its terms.

Example 1 Factorise $6a - 18b$

6 is a factor of $6a$ and $18b$ because $6a \div 6 = a$ and $18b \div 6 = 3b$.
So $6a - 18b$ factorised is $6(a - 3b)$.

Example 2 Factorise $4a^2x + 2a$

2 and a are both factors of $4a^2x$ and $2a$ since $4a^2x \div 2a = 2ax$ and $2a \div 2a = 1$.
So $4a^2x + 2a = 2a(2ax + 1)$

59

Four terms

$ax + ay + bx + by$ has four terms.
First factorise the first pair of terms and then factorise the second pair:

$ax + ay + bx + by = a(x + y) + b(x + y)$

These two terms have a common factor, $(x + y)$.
Take out $(x + y)$: $a(x + y) + b(x + y) = (a + b)(x + y)$

Example Factorise (a) $ax + ab + 2x + 2b$ (b) $x^2 + xy - 2x - 2y$

(a) $ax + ab + 2x + 2b = a(x + b) + 2(x + b) = (a + 2)(x + b)$
(b) $x^2 + xy - 2x - 2y = x(x + y) - 2(x + y) = (x - 2)(x + y)$

Factorising quadratics

When factorised, $x^2 + 7x + 12$ is in the form $(x + a)(x + b)$. What are the numbers a and b?

$(x + a)(x + b) = x^2 + (a + b)x + ab$

This has to match $x^2 + 7x + 12$.   The sum of the numbers, $(a + b)$, is 7.
                                        The product of the numbers, ab, is 12.

There are many possible pairs of whole numbers with a sum of 7, but there are only a few pairs with a product of 12.

Since their product is positive, the numbers are either both positive or both negative.

Since their sum is positive, the two numbers are positive.

The possible number pairs are 1 and 12, 2 and 6, 3 and 4.

3 and 4 have a sum of 7, so the required numbers are 3 and 4.

$x^2 + 7x + 12 = (x + 3)(x + 4)$

Example 1   Factorise $x^2 - 11x + 18$

When factorised, $x^2 - 11x + 18$ is in the form $(x + a)(x + b) = x^2 + (a + b)x + ab$.
This has to match $x^2 - 11x + 18$.   The sum of the numbers, $(a + b)$, is -11.
                                         The product of the numbers, ab, is 18.

Many pairs of whole numbers have a sum of -11; only a few have a product of 12.

Since their product is positive, the numbers are either both positive or both negative.

Since their sum is negative, the two numbers are negative.

The possible number pairs are -1 and -18, -2 and -9, -3 and -6.

-2 and -9 have a sum of -11, so the required numbers are -2 and -9.

$x^2 - 11x + 18 = (x - 2)(x - 9)$

Example 2   Factorise $x^2 - 2x - 15$

Two numbers with sum -2 and product -15 are needed.

The product is negative, so one number is positive, one is negative.

Possible number pairs with a product of −15 are:

    1, − 15   Sum is − 14, so these are not the numbers.
    3, − 5   Sum is − 2, so 3 and − 5 are the numbers.
    $x^2 − 2x − 15 = (x − 5)(x + 3)$

Example 3   Factorise $x^2 + x − 20$

We need two numbers with sum +1 and product −20.
The product is negative so one number is positive, one is negative.
Possible number pairs with a product of −20 are:

    1, − 20   Sum is − 19, so these are not the numbers.
    4, − 5   Sum is − 1, so these are not the numbers.
    − 4, 5   Sum is 1, so − 4 and 5 are the numbers.
    $x^2 + x − 20 = (x + 5)(x − 4)$

Squares and the difference of two squares

Reversing the result on page 59, $a^2 − b^2 = (a + b)(a − b)$. We can use this to factorise any expression that is the difference of two squares.
For example $x^2 − 64 = x^2 − 8^2 = (x + 8)(x − 8)$
                   $4m^2 − 25n^2 = (2m)^2 − (5n)^2 = (2m + 5n)(2m − 5n)$

Algebraic fractions

The rules for working with algebraic fractions are the same as for ordinary fractions.

Adding and subtracting

To add or subtract algebraic fractions, find equivalent fractions with a common denominator and add (or subtract) the numerators. For example,

(a) $\dfrac{x}{2} − \dfrac{y}{3} = \dfrac{3x}{6} − \dfrac{2y}{6} = \dfrac{3x − 2y}{6}$ (b) $\dfrac{2}{x} − \dfrac{1}{y} = \dfrac{2y}{xy} − \dfrac{1x}{xy} = \dfrac{2y − x}{xy}$

(c) $\dfrac{x+1}{3} − \dfrac{x−2}{4} = \dfrac{4(x+1)}{3 \times 4} − \dfrac{3(x−2)}{3 \times 4}$

            $= \dfrac{4x+4}{12} − \dfrac{3x−6}{12} = \dfrac{4x+4−3x+6}{12} = \dfrac{x+10}{12}$

Multiplying

Multiply top and bottom separately. Cancel if possible.

$$\dfrac{5x^2}{2y^2z} \times \dfrac{8y^2z^2}{10x^3} = \dfrac{\cancel{8}^1 x^2}{\cancel{2}y^2z} \times \dfrac{\cancel{8}^4 y^2 z^2}{\cancel{10}x^3}{}_2 = \dfrac{\cancel{x}^2}{\cancel{x}^2 \cancel{z}} \times \dfrac{\cancel{4}^2 \cancel{y}^2 z^{\cancel{2}}}{\cancel{2}x^{\cancel{3}}} {}_1 = \dfrac{2z}{x}$$

Dividing

The second fraction is turned upside-down and multiplied.

$$\frac{5xy}{9} \div \frac{10x^2y^2}{27} = \frac{5xy}{9} \times \frac{27}{10x^2y^3} = \frac{{}^1\cancel{5xy}}{\cancel{9}_1} \times \frac{\cancel{27}^3}{\cancel{10}_2 x^2 y^{\cancel{3}2}} = \frac{3}{2xy^2}$$

Sometimes it is necessary to factorise:

$$\frac{x^2+x}{4x} \div \frac{3x+3}{8} = \frac{x^2+x}{4x} \times \frac{8}{3x+3} = \frac{x(x+1)}{4x} \times \frac{8}{3(x+1)} = \frac{\cancel{x(x+1)}}{\cancel{4}_1 \cancel{x}} \times \frac{\cancel{8}^2}{3\cancel{(x+1)}} = \frac{2}{3}$$

Changing the subject of a formula

The method used to change the subject of a formula is very similar to the method used to solve an equation.

Example 1

The area of a trapezium is given by the formula $A = \frac{1}{2}(a+b)h$. Make b the subject of the formula.

Solve the equation $12 = \frac{1}{2}(5+b)3$

Put b on the left-hand side. $\frac{1}{2}(a+b)h = A$ $\frac{1}{2}(5+b)3 = 12$

Remove the denominator by multiplying both sides by 2. $(a+b)h = 2A$ $(5+b)3 = 12 \times 2$

Multiply out the bracket. $ah + bh = 2A$ $15 + 3b = 24$

Put the term in b alone, on one side of the equation. $bh = 2A - ah$ $3b = 24 - 15$

Divide both sides to give b. $b = \dfrac{2A - ah}{h}$ $b = \dfrac{24-15}{3}$

$$= \frac{9}{3} = 3$$

Example 2 $t = \dfrac{ax}{a+x}$

(a) Make a the subject of the formula.

(b) Calculate the value of a if $t = 4$ and $x = 12$.

(a) Multiply both sides by $(a+x)$ to remove the denominator. $t(a+x) = ax$

Multiply out the brackets. $ta + tx = ax$

Subtract ta from both sides so that the terms in a are together. $tx = ax - at$

Factorise, as a has to be on its own. $tx = a(x-t)$

Divide both sides by $(x-t)$. $a = \dfrac{xt}{x-t}$

(b) $a = \dfrac{xt}{x-t} = \dfrac{12 \times 4}{12-4} = \dfrac{48}{8} = 6$

ALGEBRAIC EXPRESSIONS AND FORMULAE – TYPICAL QUESTIONS

1   Write these expressions without brackets.
(a) $5(a + 2b)$ (b) $x(x - y)$ (c) $2x(x^2 + 3x - 1)$ (d) $2x(3x^2 - 5x + 1)$

2   Simplify these expressions.
(a) $2(x - y) + 2(x - 7y)$ (b) $5(2c - 3) - 2(c - 1)$ (c) $5x - 3 - (2x - 7)$

3   Remove the brackets in each of these expressions.
(a) $(x - 3)(x + 8)$ (b) $(2x - 1)(x + 6)$ (c) $(3x - 3y)(4x + y)$
(d) $(x - 7)^2$ (e) $(2x + 5)^2$ (f) $(4x - 1)^2$

4   Remove the brackets and simplify these expressions.
(a) $(x + 3)(x - 3)$ (b) $(2y + 4)(2y - 4)$ (c) $(5x - 3y)(5x + 3y)$

5   Simplify (a) $(4x - 1)^2 - (2x - 1)^2$ (b) $(3x + 2)^2 - (3x + 1)^2$
(c) $(x + 3)(3x - 4) - 2x(x + 1)$ (d) $(3m - 2n)^2 - (2m + 3n)(3m - n)$

6   Factorise these expressions completely.
(a) $5a - 35$ (b) $5a^2 - 2a$ (c) $6ab - 9a^2$
(d) $15abc + 5a^2$ (e) $6a + 9b - 12c$ (f) $4x + 4y - 12$
(g) $8xy - 2x^2 + 6x$ (h) $3ax - 6ay + 9az$

7   Find pairs of numbers with the following sums and products:

	Sum	Product		Sum	Product
(a)	−3	−4	(b)	−18	−40
(c)	1	−42	(d)	−16	60

8   Factorise these expressions.
(a) $x^2 + 12x + 11$ (b) $x^2 + 19x + 60$ (c) $x^2 + 9x + 20$
(d) $x^2 + 11x + 30$ (e) $x^2 - 12x + 35$ (f) $x^2 - 25x + 84$
(g) $x^2 - 2x + 1$ (h) $x^2 - 20x + 64$ (i) $x^2 + 8x - 20$
(j) $x^2 - 9x - 10$ (k) $x^2 - 14x - 51$ (l) $x^2 + 11x - 60$
(m) $3x^2 - 12$ (n) $4x^2 - 100$ (o) $a^2b^2 - 121$
(p) $9x^2 - 25y^2z^2$

9   Simplify these expressions.

(a) $\dfrac{3}{a} + \dfrac{5}{2a}$ (b) $\dfrac{3}{b} - \dfrac{2}{c}$ (c) $\dfrac{x - 2}{5} + \dfrac{x + 1}{2}$ (d) $\dfrac{2x + 3}{3} - \dfrac{x - 2}{2}$

(e) $\dfrac{2}{x} - \dfrac{1}{x^2}$ (f) $\dfrac{2a^2}{3b^3c} \times \dfrac{9b^2c}{10a}$ (g) $\dfrac{5pq}{7z^2} \div \dfrac{14p^3q^4}{20z^3}$ (h) $\dfrac{x^2 - 2x}{3} \div \dfrac{4x - 8}{9}$

10   Make the letter in brackets the subject of each of these formulae.
(a) $A = \pi r^2 h$ (r) (b) $E = \frac{1}{2}mv^2$ (m) (c) $V = 2a + 3b$ (a)

11   Use your answer to question 10(b) to calculate the value of m when $v = 4$ and $E = 8$.

12   Make r the subject of the formula $I = \dfrac{2E}{R + 2r}$. Calculate r if $E = 20$, $I = 5$ and $R = 1$.

Unit 12
SIMULTANEOUS EQUATIONS AND INEQUALITIES

Two numbers have a sum of 80 and a difference of 46. What are the numbers? If the numbers are called x and y, the two sentences can be written as:

$x + y = 80$ ….. equation (**1**)

$x - y = 24$ ….. equation (**2**)

These are a pair of **simultaneous equations**. Solving them means finding the values of x and y which make both true simultaneously. They can be solved algebraically in two ways: by **elimination of one variable** or by **substitution**.

Solving by elimination

Adding these two equations together, $\qquad x + y + x - y = 80 + 24$

Simplifying, $\qquad\qquad\qquad\qquad\qquad\qquad\qquad 2x = 104$

y has been eliminated from the equation. The only variable in it now is x.

Dividing both sides by 2, $\qquad\qquad\qquad\qquad\qquad x = 52$

Substitute for $x = 52$ in equation (**1**): $52 + y = 80$, so $y = 80 - 52 = 28$

The first equation was used to find y. Check the answer is correct by substituting the solution in the second equation. The difference is $52 - 28 = 24$ so the solution is correct. The equations could have been subtracted to find the correct answer:

$x + y - (x - y) = 80 - 24$

$x + y - x + y = 56$, so $2y = 56$ and $y = 28$

Usually, the coefficients of the two variables are different in the two equations. Multiply the two equations by suitable numbers so that they have the same coefficient for one of the variables. Eliminate this variable and find the value of the other.

Example 1 Solve these simultaneous equations.

$2m = 7 + 3n$ …..(**1**)

$5m = 4n + 14$ …..(**2**)

Step 1 Rearrange the equations so that they are in the form $am + bn = c$

(This step is not needed when $\qquad\qquad 2m - 3n = 7$ …..(**3**)

the equations are in the correct form.) $5m - 4n = 14$ …..(**4**)

64

Step 2   Multiply the two equations by suitable numbers so that the coefficients of an unknown in both equations are the same.

In this example, multiply every term in **(3)** by 4 (the coefficient of n in the other equation) and every term in **(4)** by 3.

$\quad$ **(3)** $\times$ 4: $8m - 12n = 28$ .....**(5)**

$\quad$ **(4)** $\times$ 3: $15m - 12n = 42$ .....**(6)**

Step 3   Add or subtract the equations to eliminate the terms with the same coefficient. Add if the numbers have different signs. Subtract if the signs are the same.

The term in n in both equations is the same, $-12n$. Subtract one equation from the other and the terms in n disappear. Work out **(6)** – **(5)** to keep the coefficient of m positive.

$\quad 7m - 0n = 14$

Step 4   Solve the equation with one letter in it.

$\quad 7m = 14$

$\quad\ m = 2$

Step 5   Substitute this value in equation **(1)** to find the value of the other letter.

Substituting 2 for m in **(1)**: $4 = 7 + 3n,$ $-3 = 3n$ and $n = -1$

Step 6   Check that you have not made a mistake by substituting the pair of values in **(4)**. (If you have made a mistake, go through your working to find the error.)

Substitute $m = 2$ and $n = -1$ in **(4)**: LHS = $5 \times 2 - 4 \times (-1) = 14 =$ RHS

Some word problems lead to simultaneous equations.

Example 2   I bought 5 drinks and 4 buns for \$22. My friend bought 4 drinks and 2 buns for \$14. How much do 1 bun and 1 drink each cost?

Let 1 drink cost \$$d$ and 1 bun cost \$$b$. Write the sentences in the question as equations.

I bought 5 drinks and 4 buns for \$22.	$5d + 4b = 22$.....**(1)**
My friend bought 4 drinks and 2 buns for \$14.	$4d + 2b = 14$.....**(2)**
Solve by elimination: **(2)** $\times$ 2	$8d + 4b = 28$.....**(3)**
(3) – (1)	$3d = 6$
	$d = 2$
Substitute in equation **(1)**:	$10 + 4b = 22$
	So $4b = 22 - 10 = 12$
	and $b = 3$

So a drink costs \$2 and a bun costs \$3.

Check in the original statement of the problem: 5 drinks and 4 buns cost \$10 + \$12 = \$22.

4 drinks and 2 buns cost \$8 + \$6 = \$14, as stated in the question.

Solving by substitution

Simultaneous equations can also be solved by making one variable the subject of an equation and substituting for it in the other equation.

Example   Solve these simultaneous equations. $x + y = 6$ .....**(1)**
$2x - 3y = 2$ .....**(2)**

Step 1   Use one equation to make one of the letters the subject.
From **(1)**, $x = 6 - y$

Step 2   Substitute this formula in the other equation.
Substitute $x = 6 - y$ in **(2)**: $2(6 - y) - 3y = 2$

Step 3   Solve the equation to find the value of the letter in it.
$12 - 2y - 3y = 2$
$12 - 5y = 2$
$12 = 2 + 5y$
$12 - 2 = 5y$
$10 = 5y$ so $y = 2$

Step 4   Substitute this value in equation **(1)** to find the value of the other letter.
$x + 2 = 6$ so $x = 6 - 2 = 4$

Step 5   Check your answer.   In **(2)**, LHS $= 2 \times 4 - 3 \times 2 = 2 =$ RHS
When no term has a coefficient of 1, it is usually simpler to solve by elimination.

Inequalities

These symbols are used to show inequality:

> means 'greater than'   < means 'less than'
≥ means 'greater than or equal to'   ≤ means 'less than or equal to'

The number at the big end of the symbol is the bigger number: $5 > 4$ and $4 < 5$.
Inequalities can be shown on the number line. For example, if x is a real number and $x > -1$, then x is any number greater than -1. This is shown like this:

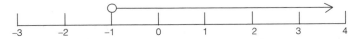

The **empty circle** shows that -1 **is not included**. The arrow shows that the line does not end. Any number to the right of -1 is > -1.

If x is a real number and $x < 2$, then x is any number less than 2:

Any number to the left of 2 is < 2. Any number to the right of 2 is greater than 2.

$\frac{1}{2} > -99$ because $\frac{1}{2}$ is to the right of -99.

$-700 < 3$ because -700 is to the left of 3 on the line.

If x is a real number and $x \leq 3$, then x is any number less than or equal to 3:

The **solid circle** shows that 3 **is included**.

If x is a real number and $x > -2$, then x is any number greater than -2. The empty circle shows that -2 is not included.

If x is a real number and $-2 \leq x < 1$, then x is any number greater than or equal to -2 and less than 1. -2 is included but 1 is not. This is shown on the number line like this:

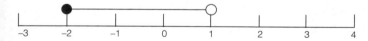

If x is an integer and $-3 \leq x < 2$, then x is any integer greater than or equal to -3 and less than 2. The integers that satisfy this condition are $-3, -2, -1, 0$ and 1. They are shown on the number line like this:

Solving inequalities is just like solving equations.

For example:

$$3(2x + 6) = 30 \qquad\qquad 3(2x + 6) < 30$$
$$6x + 18 = 30 \qquad\qquad 6x + 18 < 30$$
$$6x = 30 - 18 \qquad\qquad 6x < 30 - 18$$
$$6x = 12 \qquad\qquad 6x < 12$$
$$x = \frac{12}{6} = 2 \qquad\qquad x < \frac{12}{6} = 2$$

But when **dividing by a negative number**, turn the inequality round:

$6 > 4$ but $-6 < -4$

For example:
$$3x \le 7x + 8$$
$$3x - 7x \le 8$$
$$-4x \le 8$$
$$x \ge \frac{8}{-4} \quad \text{and} \quad x \ge -2$$

SIMULTANEOUS EQUATIONS AND INEQUALITIES – TYPICAL QUESTIONS

1 Solve the following pairs of simultaneous equations by the elimination method.

(a) $e - f = 2$ (b) $12c + d = 8$ (c) $2k + 3n = 7$ (d) $5u - 3v = -4$
     $3e - f = 10$ $3c - d = 7$ $3k + 9n = 12$ $10u - 5v = -5$

2 Solve the following pairs of simultaneous equations by the substitution method.

(a) $e = f + 1$ (b) $c = 2d + 3$ (c) $e = 2h - 4$ (d) $g - h = 5$
     $2e + 3f = 7$ $3c + d = 2$ $2e - 3h = -5$ $4g + 3h = 6$

3 Put $<$, $=$ or $>$ between each of these number pairs to make a true statement:

(a) 8   5   (b) 5   17   (c) -3 -5 (d) -44 4   (e) 4.75 $4\frac{3}{4}$

4 Solve these inequalities.

(a) $3(x + 3) < 15$ (b) $5x - 8 \ge 15$ (c) $2y - 7 \le 15$ (d) $\frac{1}{2}x - 3 > 8$
(e) $11 - 3y < 2$ (f) $5 + 4x > -3$ (g) $3 + 5x \le 13$ (h) $5 \ge 9 - 4x$

5 (a) Copy the diagram and show $x \ge -2$ on the number line.

(b) x is a real number. Show $x < 2$ on a copy of this number line.

(c) x is a natural number. Show $0 < x \le 2$ on a copy of this number line.

(d) x is an integer. Show $-2 < x \le 2$ on a copy of this number line.

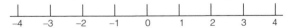

6 Two numbers have a sum of 180 and a difference of 20. Form two simultaneous equations and find the numbers.

7 I bought 3 CDs and 2 cassettes for $36. My friend bought 5 CDs and 3 cassettes for $58. How much do 1 CD and 1 cassette each cost?

Unit 13
COORDINATES AND GRAPHS

Coordinates

Coordinates are used to describe the position of points. The diagram below shows a grid of horizontal and vertical lines. The thick horizontal line across the page is the **x-axis**. The thick vertical line is the **y-axis**. The point where they meet is the **origin**, O. Point A is 4 along from O in the horizontal x direction and 2 up in the vertical y direction. The **x-coordinate** of A is 4 and the **y-coordinate** is 2. The **coordinates** of A are (4, 2).

EXAM TIP	
It is important that the coordinates are written in the correct order.	

Change the order and the point is changed. Point B has coordinates (2, 4).

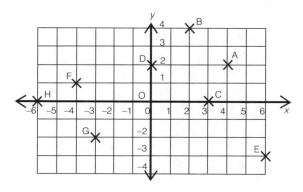

The **y-coordinate** of points on the **x-axis** is zero, e.g. C = (3, 0).
The **x-coordinate** of points on the **y-axis** is zero, e.g. D = (0, 2).

The y-coordinates of points below the x-axis are negative, e.g. E = (6, –3) .
The x-coordinates of points to the left of the y-axis are negative, e.g. F = (–4, 1).

Some other examples: G = (–3, –2), H = (–6, 0), the origin O = (0, 0).

The above diagram shows 1 cm to 1 unit.

For bigger numbers on the axes, 1 cm can represent any number. In this diagram,
1 cm represents 5 units on the x-axis and
1 cm represents 10 units on the y-axis.

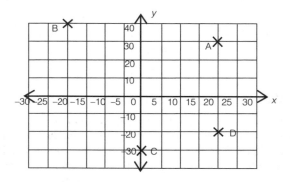

A = (20, 30), B = (−20, 40),
C = (0, −30) and D = (20, −20).

Graphs in practical situations

Conversion graphs

Conversion graphs are used to change units. For example, if 5 gallons of liquid is equivalent to 23 litres, this can be shown on a graph. A line is drawn from (0, 0) to (5, 23).

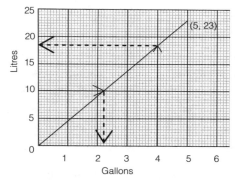

To find out how many gallons is equivalent to 10 litres, go across from 10 on the litres scale to the line and then go vertically down to approximately 2.2 on the gallons scale.

10 litres of liquid is equivalent to approximately 2.2 gallons of liquid.

To find how many litres of liquid are equivalent to 4 gallons, go up from 4 on the gallons scale to the line and then go across to 18.4 on the litres scale.

Travel graphs

A travel graph tells the story of a journey. A distance–time graph tells us the distance travelled and the time taken. The graph has distance and time axes. From the graph, you can work out the average speed travelled by using the formula:

$$\text{Average speed} = \frac{\textbf{Total distance travelled}}{\textbf{Time taken}}$$

The method of reading a travel graph is similar to the method of reading the conversion graph above. An example shows how it is done.

Example 1 Ali, Siti and Salleh live 12 km from their school. They travel to school using different kinds of transport. One travels by bus, one by car and one by bicycle. Ali takes 15 minutes to reach home from school, Siti takes 25 minutes and Salleh takes 36 minutes.

The graph shows their journeys.

Who is travelling by bus? How do you know? Who is travelling by car? And who cycles to school? What is their average speed (to the nearest km/h)?

The journey which takes the least time is the fastest journey. This also has the steepest graph. So Ali is travelling fastest, Siti is next fastest and Salleh is slowest. So Siti travels to school by bus, Ali travels to school by car and Salleh cycles.

Siti's average speed = $\dfrac{\text{Total distance travelled}}{\text{Total time}}$

$= 12 \text{ km} \div 25 \text{ min} = 12 \text{ km} \div \frac{25}{60} \text{ hr}$

$= 12 \times \frac{60}{25} \text{ km/h} = 28.8 \text{ km/h}$

Ali's average speed $= 12 \times \frac{60}{15} \text{ km/h} = 48 \text{ km/h}$

Salleh's average speed $= 12 \times \frac{60}{36} \text{ km/h} = 20 \text{ km/h}$

Example 2 Another day, Ali and Siti travelled 60 km to Bandar Seri Begawan by car to do some shopping. Their journeys are shown on the graph. Describe Ali's and Siti's journeys. At what time do they meet for the second time?

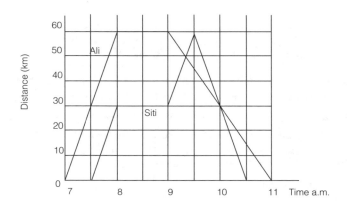

Ali left home at 7 a.m. and reached Bandar Seri Begawan 60 km away at 8 a.m. His speed was 60 km/h. He stayed in Bandar Seri Begawan for 1 hour until 9 a.m. He drove back home, arriving 2 hours later at 11 a.m.
His average speed for the return journey was $\frac{60}{2}$ km/h = 30 km/h.
Siti left home at 7.30 a.m. and travelled 30 km by 8 a.m. She stopped until 9 a.m.
Her speed was $\frac{30}{\frac{1}{2}}$ km/h = 60 km/h.

At 9 a.m. she left for Bandar Seri Begawan at the same speed, arriving at 9.30 a.m. She then drove home, arriving one hour later at 10.30 p.m.
Her speed on the return journey was $\frac{60}{1}$ km/h = 60 km/h.

They met at 10 a.m.

Graphs of linear equations
Vertical lines

$x = -2$ is a vertical line through $(-2, 0)$.
Every point on this line has x-coordinate -2.

> The y-axis has equation $x = 0$.
> $x = a$ is a vertical line through $(a, 0)$.
> Every point on $x = a$ has x-coordinate a.

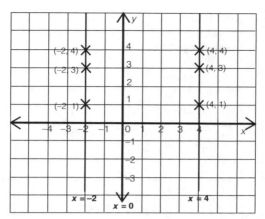

Horizontal lines

$y = 2$ is a horizontal line through $(0, 2)$.
Every point on this line has y-coordinate 2.

> **The x-axis has equation $y = 0$.**
> **$y = a$ is a horizontal line through $(0, a)$.**
> **Every point on $y = a$ has y-coordinate a.**

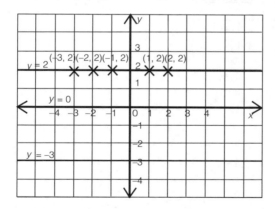

Sloping lines through the origin

Graphs of the type $y = ax$ where a is a constant are straight-line graphs.
The **coordinates** of the graph can be obtained from sets of values of y and x.

For example, $y = 3x$ $\qquad\qquad$ $y = -2x$

x	−2	0	1	2	3
$y = 3x$	−6	0	3	6	9

x	−1	0	1	2	3
$y = -2x$	2	0	−2	−4	−6

So the line $y = 3x$ goes through $(0, 0)$, $(1, 3)$, $(2, 6)$, $(3, 9)$.
The line $y = -2x$ goes through $(0, 0)$, $(1, -2)$, $(2, -4)$, $(3, -6)$.
The lines are shown on this graph:

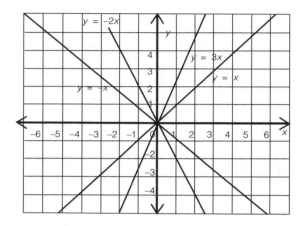

Example   Draw the graph of $2x + y = 6$

Prepare a table of values, after rearranging the equation so that $y = 6 - 2x$.
The calculation can be done in the table.

x	0	1	2	3
$2x$	0	2	4	6
$y = 6 - 2x$	6	4	2	0

The graph is:

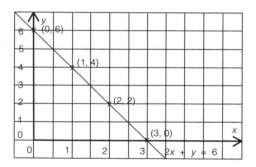

Other sloping lines

> **The equation of a straight line with gradient m and y-intercept at $(c, 0)$**
> (this means that $(c, 0)$ is the point where the line crosses the y-axis) **is**
> $y = mx + c$.

For example, the equation of the line with gradient $m = \frac{1}{2}$ and y-intercept 3 is $y = \frac{1}{2}x + 3$

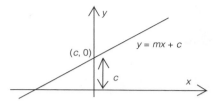

Solving simultaneous equations by graphing

A pair of simultaneous equations can be solved by drawing their graph. The solution is the coordinates of the point where the two graphs intersect. The graph of the lines can be drawn by preparing a table of values for a few points. As each line is straight, you only need to plot a few points to be able to draw the line.

Example On the same axes, for values of x from 0 to 4, draw the graphs of $y = 2x - 1$ and $2y + 3x = 12$ and hence solve these equations simultaneously.

Rearrange $2y + 3x = 12$. Dividing both sides by 2, $y + \frac{3}{2}x = 6$, so $y = 6 - \frac{3}{2}x$

The tables of values for these two lines are:

x	0	2	4
$2x$	0	4	8
$y = 2x - 1$	−1	3	7

x	0	2	4
$\frac{3}{2}x$	0	3	6
$y = 6 - \frac{3}{2}x$	6	3	0

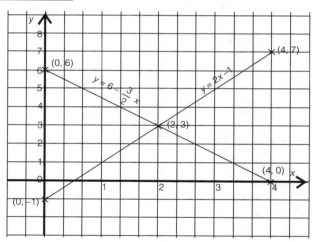

The graphs meet at (2, 3).
The solution of the pair of simultaneous equations is
$x = 2$, $y = 3$.

Gradient of a straight line

The gradient (m) of the line joining points A (x_1, y_1) and B (x_2, y_2) is $m = \dfrac{y_2 - y_1}{x_2 - x_1}$

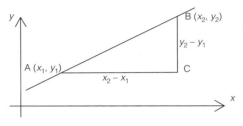

Negative gradient $m < 0$ **Zero gradient** $m = 0$ **Positive gradient** $m > 0$

Example Find the equation of the straight line through A = (3, 2) and B = (6, –4).

The gradient AB is $m = \dfrac{-4 - 2}{6 - 3} = \dfrac{-6}{3} = -2$

So the line is $y = 2x + c$ and passes through (3, 2).
Substituting, $2 = -2 \times 3 + c$ so $2 = -6 + c$ and $c = 8$
So the equation is $y = 2x + 8$, which can also be written as $y + 2x = 8$

Length and mid-point of a line segment

In the diagram above, A = (x_1, y_1), and B = (x_2, y_2).
By Pythagoras' theorem, $AB^2 = AC^2 + BC^2$. $AC^2 = (x_2 - x_1)^2$ and $BC^2 = (y_2 - y_1)^2$.

So the **length of AB** = $\sqrt{(x_2 - x_1)^2 + (y_2 - y_1)^2}$

The **mid-point of AB** is $\left(\dfrac{x_1 + x_2}{2}, \dfrac{y_1 + y_2}{2} \right)$

Example

(a) Calculate the length of AB if A (2, 4) and B (8, 12).
(b) Find the mid-point of AB.

(a) AB = $\sqrt{((8 - 2)^2 + (12 - 4)^2)}$
$= \sqrt{(36 + 64)} = \sqrt{100} = 10$

(b) The mid-point of AB = $\left(\dfrac{2 + 8}{2}, \dfrac{4 + 12}{2} \right) = (5, 8)$

COORDINATES AND GRAPHS – TYPICAL QUESTIONS

1 A = (2, 2), B = (4, 8). Calculate
   (a) the distance AB   (b) the equation of the line AB
   (c) the gradient of AB.

2 P = (5, 9) and Q = (11, 6). Find
   (a) the length of PQ   (b) the mid-point of PQ
   (c) the equation of the line PQ.

3 ABCD is a parallelogram. A = (4, 3), B = (8, 6), C = (9, 9). What are the coordinates of D?

4 (a) Complete this table and draw the graph of $y = 2x + 1$.

x	-2	-1	0	1	2
$y = 2x + 1$					

   (b) On the same axes, draw the line $x + y = 4$.
   (c) Solve the simultaneous equations $y = 2x + 1$ and $x + y = 4$.

5 (a) The line $y = \frac{1}{3}x + c$ passes through the point (6, –2). Find c.
   (b) Find the gradient and the y-intercept of the line $3y - x = 8$.
   (c) A = (–1, 5) and B = (6, 5). What is the equation of the line AB?

6 This table shows the charges for using the telephone for long distance calls to West Malaysia.

Minutes	0–3	4	6	8	10	12
Charge (B$)	6.30	8.40	12.60	16.80	21.00	23.10

   (a) Draw a graph to represent this table. On the vertical axis use a scale of $8 to 2 cm, and on the horizontal axis use a scale of 2 minutes to 1 cm.
   (b) Use your graph to find
      (i) the charge for calling for 11 minutes
      (ii) how many minutes you have called if you are charged $14.70.

7 Draw a pair of axes such that the x-axis is from –6 to 6 and y-axis is from –4 to 4.
   (a) On the Cartesian plane, plot the points A (–4, 1) and B (2, 3). Join these points with a straight line.
   (b) Plot the point C (3, 1) and draw a line through C parallel to AB.
   (c) Write down the coordinates of another point on this new line.

Unit 14 _____
ANGLES AND POLYGONS

Angles

An angle is an amount of turn.

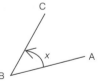

The angle marked x in the diagram is angle ABC, written $\angle$ABC or $A\hat{B}C$.
The angle is at point B which is the vertex of the angle.
Angles are measured in **degrees**. There are 360 degrees (**360°**) in a **full turn**
or **one revolution**. The sum of the angles at a point is 360°. Here are some
words used to describe angles.

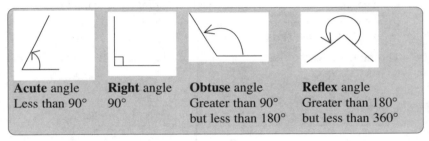

| **Acute** angle | **Right** angle | **Obtuse** angle | **Reflex** angle |
| Less than 90° | 90° | Greater than 90° but less than 180° | Greater than 180° but less than 360° |

The **right angle** is very common, seen in bricks, windows, tiles, books and
many other places.
Two lines crossing each other at right angles are **perpendicular** lines.
XY is perpendicular to AB.

This symbol means the angle
is a right angle.

Two angles which add up to 90° are **complementary**
angles. 53° + 37° = 90° so 53° and 37° are
complementary angles.

The angles on a **straight line** add up to 180°.
Two angles which add up to 180° are **supplementary**
angles. 128° + 52° = 180° so 128° and 52° are
supplementary angles.

When two straight lines intersect each other, the **vertically opposite** angles are equal.
$a = c$ and $b = d$.

Example   Calculate the value of x in these diagrams.

(a)

(b)

(a) $x + 42° = 180°$
    (angles on a straight line)
    $x = 180° - 42°$
    $= 138°$

(b) $y + 200° + 32° = 360°$
    (angles at a point)
    $y = 360° - 200° - 32°$
    $= 128°$

Measuring angles using a protractor

Angle AYX will be used as an example.
- Estimate the size of the angle – this acute angle is about 60°.
- Place the centre of the protractor **exactly on** the vertex of the angle, Y.
- Lay the base of the protractor **exactly along** the straight line AY.
- Look where the line XY is under the scale on the protractor.
- Read the size of the angle.
- There are two scales. One shows 52° and the other 128°.
- Since the angle is acute, the answer must be 52°.

Drawing angles using a protractor

For example, drawing $\angle AYX = 52°$.
- Draw a line AY.
- Place the centre of the protractor **exactly on** Y.

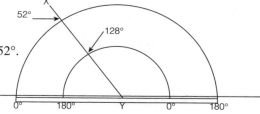

- Lay the base of the protractor **exactly along** A.
- Look on the scale on the protractor for 52°. Make a dot at the 52° mark.
- Draw a line through Y and the dot.
- Label the other end of this line X.

Parallel lines

Parallel lines are straight lines that go in the same direction.

Parallel lines in a plane never meet no matter how far they are extended (**produced**). They are indicated with arrows.

The angles that parallel lines make with lines that cross them (**transversals**) have several properties, described below.

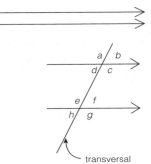

Alternate angles are equal. In the diagram above $d = f$ and $c = e$.
They make a Z-shape like this 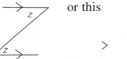 or this

Corresponding angles are equal. In the diagram above $a = e$, $b = f$, $d = h$ and $c = g$.
They make an F-shape like this 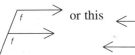 or this

Interior angles are supplementary.
They make a U-shape like this 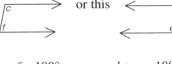 or this

$$c + f = 180° \qquad d + e = 180° \qquad r + s = 180°$$

So, when a line crosses two parallel lines, the angles are equal in two groups like this.
Also $a + b = 180°$

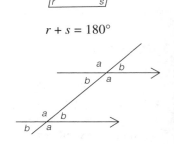

80

Example Find the sizes of the angles marked with letters in these diagrams.

(a)

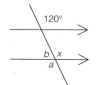

(b)

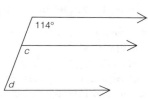

(c)

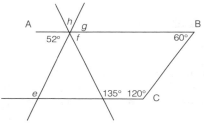

(a) $x = 120°$ (corresponding ∠s)
   $b + x = 180°$ (∠s on a straight line)
   ∴ $b = 180° - 120° = 60°$
   $a = x = 120°$ (vertically opposite ∠s)

(b) $c = 114°$ (corresponding ∠s)
   $c + d = 180°$ (interior ∠s)
   ∴ $d = 180° - 114° = 66°$

(c) Because the interior angles $60° + 120° = 180°$, lines AB and DC are parallel.
   So $e + 52° = 180°$ (interior ∠s) and $e = 128°$
   also $f + 135° = 180°$ (interior ∠s) so $f = 45°$
   $g = 52°$ (vertically opposite angles)
   $45° + 52° + h = 180°$ (angles on a straight line) so $h = 180° - 97° = 83°$

Types of triangles and polygons

A **polygon** is a shape with straight sides.
A 3-sided polygon is a **triangle**.
A 4-sided polygon is a **quadrilateral**.
A 5-sided polygon is a **pentagon**.
A 6-sided polygon is a **hexagon**.
A 7-sided polygon is a **heptagon**.
An 8-sided polygon is an **octagon**.

Triangle

Quadrilateral

Regular hexagon   Regular octagon

A 9-sided polygon is a **nonagon**.

A 10-sided polygon is a **decagon**.

A **regular polygon** has sides that are all the same length and angles that are all the same size. Squares and equilateral triangles are regular polygons.

Angle properties of triangles and quadrilaterals

The sum of the angles of a triangle is 180°.

An **exterior angle** of a triangle is made by lengthening (**producing**) one side. In the diagram, AC has been produced to D.

Angle BCD is an exterior angle of ABC.

An exterior angle of a triangle is equal to the sum of the two interior opposite angles of the triangle.

Exterior angle BCD = ∠BAC + ∠ABC

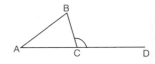

An **isosceles triangle** has two sides the same length, two angles the same size and one line of symmetry.

Isosceles triangle

line of symmetry

An **equilateral triangle** has all three sides equal and all angles equal to 60°.

An equilateral triangle has 3 lines of symmetry and order of rotational symmetry 3. (See Unit 16 on symmetry.)

Equilateral triangle

The angles and sides of a **scalene** triangle are all different sizes. It has no line of symmetry and no rotational symmetry.

An **obtuse-angled triangle** has one angle obtuse (more than 90°).

Obtuse–angled triangle

All the angles of an **acute-angled** triangle are acute (less than 90°).

Acute–angled triangle

The sum of the angles of a quadrilateral is 360°.

(Quadrilaterals can be divided into two triangles. Therefore the sum of the angles of a quadrilateral = 2 × 180° = 360°.)

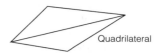

Quadrilateral

Properties of squares and rectangles

Squares have all sides the same length. All angles are right angles.
The diagonals bisect each other at right angles and are equal in length.

Square

Rectangles have opposite sides equal and all angles are right angles.
The diagonals bisect each other and are the same length.
AC = BD   so AO = BO = CO = DO

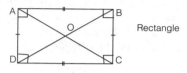

Rectangle

Properties of parallelograms and rhombuses

A parallelogram is made when two pairs of parallel lines meet.
All **parallelograms** have opposite sides equal in length and parallel. Opposites angles are also equal.

Parallelogram

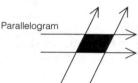

Rhombuses are parallelograms with all sides equal in length.
They can be made from two congruent isosceles triangles.
Opposites angles are equal. The diagonals bisect each other at right angles.

Rhombus

Properties of kites and trapezia

Kites have two pairs of adjacent sides equal.
In the diagram, AB = AC and BD = CD.
They can be made from two isosceles triangles with the same base.
One diagonal bisects the other.

Kite

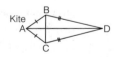

A **trapezium** has one pair of sides parallel to each other.

Trapezium

Angle properties of polygons

A polygon has **interior** and **exterior** angles.

A polygon with n sides can be divided into $(n - 2)$ triangles.

So the formula for the **sum of the interior angles** in a polygon with n sides is $(n - 2) \times 180°$ or $(2n - 4) \times 90°$.

The **sum of the exterior angles** is always $360°$.

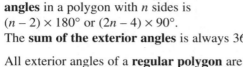

All exterior angles of a **regular polygon** are equal to $\dfrac{360°}{\text{number of sides}} = \dfrac{360°}{n}$

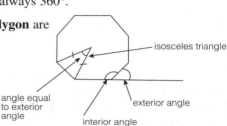

Interior angle + exterior angle = $180°$

The interior angles of a regular polygon are $180°$ – exterior angle = $180° - \dfrac{360°}{n}$

REVISION TIP

Write down all these – parallelogram, rhombus, kite, trapezium, sum of interior and exterior angles of polygon, angles of a regular polygon.

Close your book. Write down what you know about all of them. Open the book and check if you are correct.

ANGLES AND POLYGONS – TYPICAL QUESTIONS

1   How many degrees are there in
    (a) $\frac{2}{3}$ of a revolution   (b) $\frac{3}{5}$ of a right angle?

2   (a) A triangle has angles of $x°$, $(3x - 40)°$ and $(2x + 28)°$. Find the value of x.
    (b) Two of the angles of an isosceles triangle are $(2x - 40)°$ and $(x + 20)°$. Find the possible values of x.

3   In triangle ABC, $\angle ABC = 68°$. AB is produced to D.
    $\angle ACB = 75°$. Find $\angle CAB$ and $\angle CBD$.

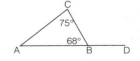

4 Find the sizes of the angles marked with letters in these diagrams.

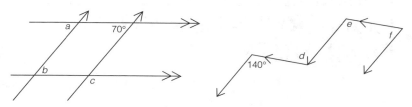

5 ABCD is a quadrilateral with angles A = x, B = $2x$, C = $3x$ and D = $4x$. Find the value of x. What kind of quadrilateral is ABCD?

6 (a) Each interior angle of a polygon is 160°. How many sides does it have?

(b) The interior angles of a quadrilateral are in the ratio 2 : 3 : 6 : 7. Find the smallest angle of the quadrilateral.

7 In the diagram, ABC and ACD are isosceles triangles in which AB = AC = AD and ∠BAC = ∠ACD = 76°.
Calculate (a) ∠CAD   (b) ∠BCA

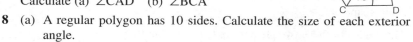

8 (a) A regular polygon has 10 sides. Calculate the size of each exterior angle.

(b) Another regular polygon has n sides. The size of each interior angle is eight times the size of each exterior angle. Find n and the size of each exterior angle.

9 ABCD is a square. X is the point on AB such that ∠AXD = 60°. Calculate ∠XDB.

10 (a) ABCD is a rhombus in which ∠ABC = 74°. Calculate ∠ACD.

(b) Four of the interior angles of a pentagon are 100°. Calculate the fifth angle.

(c) ABCDEFGH is a regular octagon with centre O.
(i) Calculate the size of one of the exterior angles of the octagon.
(ii) Calculate ∠AOD.

Unit 15 _____
CONGRUENCE AND SIMILARITY

Congruence and congruent triangles

Figures which are the same shape and size are
congruent. These two shapes are congruent.

  The two faces on the left are the same shape but they are
not congruent as they are not the same size. These
shapes are **similar.**

Corresponding lengths of these two shapes are the same
but they are not congruent because they are not the
same shape.

The angles of these two shapes are the same but they
are not congruent because the lengths are different.

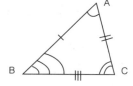 

These two triangles ABC and PQR are congruent, $\triangle ABC \equiv \triangle PQR$.
∠A equals 'corresponding' ∠P, ∠B equals corresponding ∠Q,
∠C equals corresponding ∠R.
AB = corresponding side PQ, AC = corresponding side PR,
BC = corresponding side QR.

Knowing enough to state that two triangles are congruent

You do not need to know the measures of all the sides and all the angles of two
triangles to be certain they are congruent. There are four important cases in
which less information is enough. This information is also enough to be able
to draw the triangles accurately.

Case 1 Three sides (SSS)

Two triangles are congruent if each side of one triangle is equal in length to a side of the other triangle.

ΔABC ≡Δ PQR, because AB = PQ, AC = PR and BC = QR.

Case 2 Two sides and the included angle (SAS)

Two triangles are congruent if two pairs of corresponding sides are equal in length and the angles between them are equal in size.

ΔABC ≡Δ PQR, because AB = PQ, BC = QR and ∠ABC = ∠PQR.

The angle between two lines is called the **included angle**.

Important note: If the pair of angles that are equal are **not** the included angles, then the triangles **may not** be congruent.

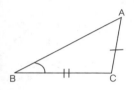 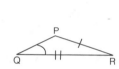

For example, in these triangles AC = PR, BC = QR and ∠B = ∠Q. But the two triangles are definitely not congruent.

Case 3 Two angles and a corresponding side (AAS)

Two triangles are congruent if two angles of one triangle equal any two angles of the other triangle and a side of one triangle is the same length as the corresponding side of the other triangle.

ΔABC ≡Δ PQR, because ∠A = ∠P, ∠C = ∠R, and BC = QR.

Case 4 Right angle, hypotenuse, side (RHS)

Two right-angled triangles are congruent if their hypotenuses are equal in length and if one side of one triangle is equal to a side of the other triangle.

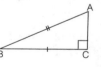 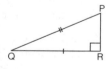

ΔABC ≡Δ PQR, because ∠C = ∠R = 90°, AB = PQ, and BC = QR.

Example ABCD is a parallelogram.
Why are triangles ABD and CDB congruent?

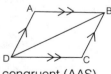

There are several ways to answer this:
1. Since AD//BC, ∠ADB = ∠DBC (alternate angles).
   Since AB//DC, ∠ABD = ∠BDC (alternate angles).
   DB is in both triangles ABD and CBD, so they are congruent (AAS).

2. AB = DC and AD = BC (opposite sides of a parallelogram).
   DB is in both triangles, so the two triangles are congruent (SSS).
3. Since AD//BC, ∠ADB = ∠DBC (alternate angles).
   AD = BC (opposite sides of a parallelogram).
   DB is in both triangles. The two triangles are congruent (SAS).

Similarity and similar triangles

Shapes whose sides are in proportion and whose
angles are equal are **similar.**
For example, these shapes are similar. The angles are the same
and the lengths of the larger one are twice the lengths of the smaller one.

Conditions for two triangles to be similar

Case 1   Two pairs of corresponding angles equal (AAA)
Draw triangles ABC and DEF with ∠A = ∠D, ∠B = ∠E and ∠C = ∠F.
Measure their sides.

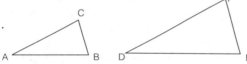

Work out $\dfrac{AB}{DE}, \dfrac{BC}{EF}, \dfrac{CA}{FD}$

They should be the same.

Corresponding sides of the two triangles are in the same ratio.They are similar.

Triangles which have the same angles are similar.
Shapes with more than three sides can have the
same angles but not be similar. For example, this
square and this rectangle have the same angles
but they are not similar.

If you know that two pairs of angles in two triangles are equal, then you know
that the third pair are equal. For example, if two angles are 28° and 80°, the
third angle in both triangles must be 180° − 28° − 80° = 72°.

Case 2   All corresponding sides in the same ratio (SSS)
If corresponding sides are in the same ratio, then the two triangles are similar.

**Case 3   Two pairs of corresponding sides in the same ratio, and included
angles equal (SAS)**

If $\dfrac{AB}{DE} = \dfrac{BC}{EF}$ and ∠B = ∠E, triangles ABC and DEF are similar.

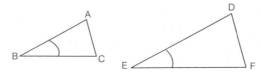

Example   In the diagram, AC//DE.
· AD = 3 cm, DB = 9 cm, and AC = 4 cm.
How long is DE?

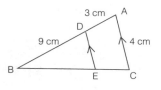

Draw a diagram with the two triangles separated.
Then it is much easier to see which are the
corresponding sides of the two triangles.

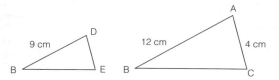

DB corresponds to AB.
DE corresponds to AC.
If DE = n cm, $\frac{n}{4} = \frac{9}{12}$.
So $n = 3$ and DE = 3 cm.

Sides, areas and volumes of similar figures

These two triangles are similar (SAS). The ratio of corresponding sides is
6 : 2 = 3 : 1.

Area of larger triangle = $\frac{1}{2} \times 6 \times 3 = 9$ sq. unit
Area of smaller triangle = $\frac{1}{2} \times 2 \times 1 = 1$ sq. unit

The ratio of the areas = $9 : 1 = 3^2 : 1^2$ = ratio of squares of sides.

This cuboid is 2 cm by 3 cm by 4 cm.   This one is 8 cm by 12 cm by 16 cm.

     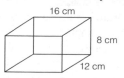

Surface area
= $2(2 \times 3 + 3 \times 4 + 4 \times 2)$ cm^2
= 52 cm^2

Surface area
= $2(8 \times 12 + 12 \times 16 + 16 \times 8)$
= 832 cm^2

Volume = $4 \times 3 \times 2$ cm^3 = 24 cm^3 Volume = $16 \times 12 \times 8$ cm^3 = 1536 cm^3

The ratio of the lengths of corresponding sides = 4 : 1
The ratio of the surface areas = $832 : 52 = 16 : 1 = 4^2 : 1$
The ratio of the volumes is $1536 : 24 = 64 : 1 = 4^3 : 1$
These results illustrate the following important rules.

> **If two similar figures are in the ratio $a : 1$, then their areas are in the
> ratio $a^2 : 1$, and their volumes are in the ratio $a^3 : 1$.**
> **If two similar figures are in the ratio $a : b$, then their areas are in the
> ratio $a^2 : b^2$, and their volumes are in the ratio $a^3 : b^3$.**

If you multiply lengths by 5, areas are multiplied by 5^2 and volumes by 5^3.

Scale drawing

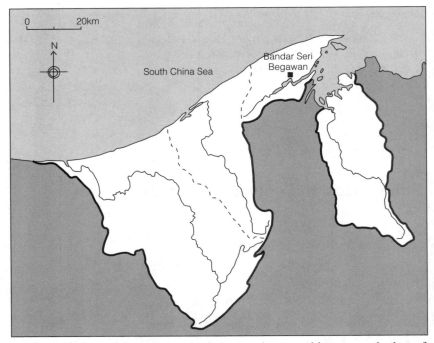

This map of Brunei Darussalam is the same shape as this country is, but of course it is much smaller. It has been drawn so that a distance of 100 km between two places is shown as a distance of 2 cm on the map.

So 2 cm on the map 'represents' 100 km on the ground

   1 cm on the map represents 50 km = 50 × 1000 × 100 cm = 5 000 000 cm

The scale of the map is 1 : 5 000 000.

Scales of maps and plans are usually stated as 1 : n. A plan of a classroom would have a smaller value of n.

Example   Suppose a plan of a classroom is 10 cm by 5.5 cm.

If the scale of the plan is 1 : 100, then the length of the actual classroom is 10 cm × 100 = 10 m and the width of the actual classroom is 5.5 cm × 100 = 5.5 m.

CONGRUENCE AND SIMILARITY – TYPICAL QUESTIONS

1   Which of these triangles are congruent to each other? Which are similar?

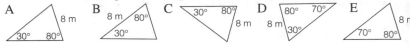

2 Triangle ABC is isosceles, with BA = BC. $\hat{ADB}$ = 90°. State the reasons that triangles ADB and CDB are congruent.

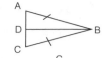

3 In the diagram, PQ//CB.
   (a) State why triangles APQ and ACB are similar.
   (b) AP = 8 cm, AC = 12 cm and AQ = 10 cm.
      (i) How long is AB?
      (ii) What is the ratio AQ : AB?
      (iii) What is the ratio of area $\triangle$AQP : area $\triangle$ABC?

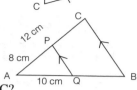

4 In the diagram, $\hat{ADE}$ = $\hat{ABC}$.
   (a) State why triangles ADE and ABC are similar.
   (b) AE = 12 cm, ED = 8 cm and BC = 16 cm.
      (i) How long is AC?
      (ii) What is the ratio of area $\triangle$ADE : area $\triangle$ABC?

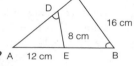

5 The ratio of the radius of circle P to the radius of circle Q is 5 : 8.
   (a) Calculate the ratio of the area of circle P to the area of circle Q.
   (b) If circle P has an area of 200 cm², what is the area of circle Q?

6 The ratio of the area of square A to the area of square B is 25 : 16.
   (a) Calculate the ratio of the length of a side of square A to the length of a side of square B.
   (b) Square A has a side of 10 cm. What is the length of a side of square B?

7 The ratio of the volume of two cubes is 27 : 8.
   (a) Calculate the ratio of lengths of the sides of the two cubes.
   (b) Calculate the ratio of surface areas of the two cubes.
   (c) The cubes are made of the same material. If the smaller cube has a mass of 16 kg, what is the mass of the larger cube?

8 The scale of a map is 1 : 200 000.
   (a) Two rivers on the map are 8 cm apart. How far apart are the actual rivers?
   (b) Two hills are 40 km apart. How far apart are they on the map?
   (c) A town on the map has an area of 6 cm². What is the area of the actual town?

9 The scale of a plan of a school is 1 : 200.
   (a) A classroom on the plan is 5 cm long. How long is the actual classroom?
   (b) Two flagpoles are 40 m apart. How far apart are they on the plan?
   (c) A room in the school has an area of 20 m². What is the area of the room on the plan?

Unit 16

SYMMETRY AND TRANSFORMATION GEOMETRY

Line and rotational symmetry

The line divides this figure into two congruent halves. A figure has **line symmetry** if you can divide it into two identical halves.

Rectangles have two **lines of symmetry**.

A shape with line symmetry can be turned over and it fits into the same space. This isosceles triangle can be turned over about its one line of symmetry and it fits into the same space.

These shapes and letters have no lines of symmetry.

 G Q P

This shape can be **rotated** (turned around) and it fits its own outline in two ways. There are two positions in which the shape looks the same. It has **rotational symmetry** of order 2.

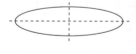

The letter **G** fits its outline in only one way. It has order of rotational symmetry 1. When a shape has rotational symmetry order 1, it has no rotational symmetry.

These shapes and letters all have rotational symmetry of order 2.

H I N  **Ø S**

The numbers of lines of symmetry of the shapes are:

  2   2   0   2   0   2   0   2

Symmetry properties of polygons and solids

Regular polygons

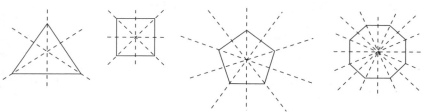

Equilateral triangle	Square	Regular pentagon	Regular octagon
3 lines of symmetry	4 lines of symmetry	5 lines of symmetry	8 lines of symmetry

Order of rotational symmetry (the number of ways it fits into its outline):

| 3 | 4 | 5 | 8 |

> **A regular *n*-sided polygon has *n* lines of symmetry and order of rotational symmetry *n*.**

Other quadrilaterals

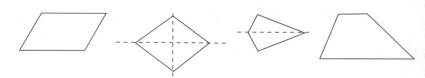

	Parallelogram	Rhombus	Kite	Trapezium
Order of rotational symmetry	2	2	1	1
Lines of symmetry	0 (**not** diagonals)	2 (diagonals)	1 (diagonal)	0

Solids

A solid has **rotational symmetry** if it can be turned less than 360° about an axis of rotation and it appears exactly the same as it did before the turn. The **order of rotational symmetry** is the number of ways this can be done. A solid has **reflection symmetry** if it can be divided into two identical halves by a plane. It has symmetry if every point can be joined to a corresponding point on the other side of the solid. Here are some examples.

Prism

 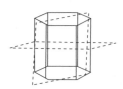

1 vertical axis   6 vertical planes
6 horizontal axes   1 horizontal plane

Cylinder

  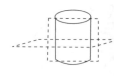

1 vertical axis   1 horizontal plane
infinite number of   infinite number of
horizontal axes   vertical planes

Pyramid

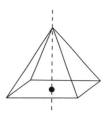

1 vertical axis   2 vertical planes

Cone

1 vertical axis   infinite number of
vertical planes

Reflections

A person who looks in a mirror sees an image of herself that is the same size as the person. In the diagram, triangle ABC is reflected onto A'B'C' in the mirror line.

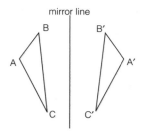

Triangle A'B'C' is the **image** of triangle ABC.

$$A \rightarrow A'$$
$$B \rightarrow B'$$
$$C \rightarrow C'$$

Triangle A'B'C' is congruent to triangle ABC:
AB = A'B', BC = B'C', CA = C'A'
A' and A are the same distance from the mirror.
The mirror line is perpendicular to AA', to BB' and to CC'.

Unlike ordinary reflection, mathematical reflection is a two-way process. In this diagram, triangle PQR is reflected in the mirror line. Its image is P'Q'R'. Q is on the side of the mirror line opposite to P and R.

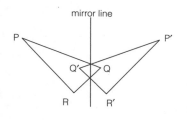

The images of P and R are on the right of the mirror line.

The image of Q is on the left of the mirror line.

Note that the triangles PQR and P'Q'R' are congruent.

PQ = P'Q', QR = Q'R', RP = R'P'.

Under a reflection, the image is congruent to the original shape.

Reflection in the Cartesian plane

Reflection in the x-axis and y-axis

If X (3, –4) is reflected in the x-axis, its image Y = (3, 4).

If X is reflected in the y-axis, its image Z = (–3, –4).

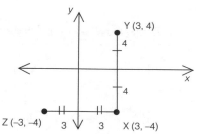

> **When reflected in the x-axis, $(x, y) \rightarrow (x, -y)$**
> **When reflected in the y-axis, $(x, y) \rightarrow (-x, y)$**

Reflection in the lines $x = a$ and $y = b$

The image A' of A (3, 4) after reflection in the line $x = 2$ is the same distance from the line $x = 2$ but on the other side of it.

A (3, 4) is 1 unit from the line, so A' = (1, 4). Note that the y-coordinate is unchanged.

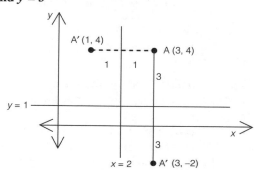

The image of A (3, 4) after reflection in the line $y = 1$ is A' (3, –2).
A (3, 4) is 3 units from the line; its image is 3 units from the line on the other side of it at A' (3, –2).
Note that the x-coordinate is unchanged.

The image of (5, –2) in the line $x = 1$ is
(2 – 5, –2) = (–3, –2).

Reflection in the lines $y = x$ and $y = -x$
When reflecting in the line $y = x$
the triangle in the diagram moves
from being on the x-axis to being on
the y-axis.
The coordinates swap over. The
image of (5, 3) is (3, 5).

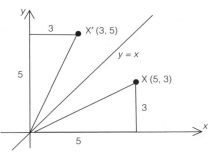

> **Under a reflection in the line $y = x$, $(x, y) \rightarrow (y, x)$**

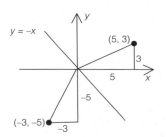

When reflecting in the line $y = -x$, the
triangle also moves from being on the x-axis
to being on the lower part of the y-axis.
The image of (5, 3) is (–3, –5).

> **Under a reflection in the line $y = -x$, $(x, y) \rightarrow (-y, -x)$**

Rotations

When an object is rotated (or turned around), it stays the same size and shape.
A shape and its image are congruent. To describe a rotation, three things are
needed:

(i) **The centre of rotation**. If a rectangle is turned about its
centre, it moves like this. The centre stays fixed.
If the rectangle is rotated about one corner, it will rotate
like this.
The rotation is quite different with a different centre of
rotation.

(ii) The angle of rotation. This triangle has experienced a quarter turn (90°).

This triangle has experienced a half-turn (180°) In both cases the centre of rotation is the mid-point of the base of the triangle.

(iii) The direction of rotation. This triangle has been rotated 90° clockwise (in the same direction as the hands of a clock) about point O. A′ is the image of A and B′ is the image of B.

This pentagon has been rotated 90° anti-clockwise.

A clockwise rotation is negative.   An anti-clockwise rotation is positive. A +270° rotation has the same effect as a –90° rotation.

In this diagram, triangle PQR is rotated –60° about centre O. This means that ∠POP′ = ∠QOQ′ = ∠ROR′ = 60°. Also OP = OP′, OQ = OQ′ and OR = OR′. **A point and its image are the same distance from the centre of rotation.** To make the diagram clearer, only OP and OP′ (thick lines), and OQ and OQ′ (dotted lines) are shown.

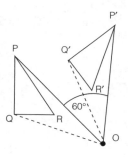

Rotation in the Cartesian plane

To find the image of a point under a rotation, draw a triangle as in the diagram.

A rotation of +90° about O
In the diagram, A (4, 3) is rotated +90° about O.
A (4, 3) → A′ (–3, 4)
$(x, y) \rightarrow (-y, x)$

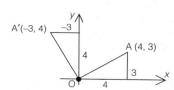

A rotation of +180° about O

In the diagram, A(4, 3) is rotated 180°
about O.

A (4, 3) → A′ (−4, −3)

(x, y) → (−x, −y)

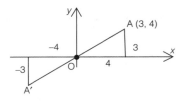

A rotation of +270° about O

In the diagram, A (4, 3) is rotated +270°
about O.

A (4, 3) → A′ (3, −4)

(x, y) → (y, −x)

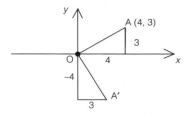

Translations and vectors

If an object slides from one place to
another without rotating, the movement is
a **translation**.

In this diagram, triangle ABC has been
translated to A′B′C′.

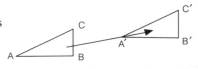

When something is translated it does not change its size.

All the points move the same distance in the same direction.

Triangle ABC and its image A′B′C′ are congruent.

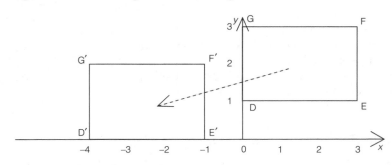

In this diagram, DEFG is translated to D′E′F′G′.

D = (0, 1), D′ = (−4, 0) = (0 − 4, 1 − 1)
E = (3, 1), E′ = (−1, 0) = (3 − 4, 0 − 1)
F = (3, 3), F′ = (−1, 2) = (3 − 4, 2 − 1)
G = (0, 3), G′ = (−4, 2) = (0 − 4, 3 − 1)

For each point, the x-coordinate changes by −4. The y-coordinate changes

by −1. The vector of the translation is $\begin{pmatrix} -4 \\ -1 \end{pmatrix}$, written vertically to avoid
confusion with (−4, −1).

Under a translation with vector $\begin{pmatrix} a \\ b \end{pmatrix}$, $(x, y) \rightarrow (x + a, y + b)$

If the image of (x, y) under a translation is (a, b) the vector of the translation is $\begin{pmatrix} a - x \\ b - y \end{pmatrix}$

Example   (a) Under a translation, the image of (5, 3) is (7, –2). What is the vector of this translation?

(b) Point A has image (3, 7) under the same translation. What are the coordinates of A?

(a) (5, 3) → (7, –2), so the vector is $\begin{pmatrix} 7 & -5 \\ -2 & -3 \end{pmatrix} = \begin{pmatrix} 2 \\ -5 \end{pmatrix}$

(b) (3, 7) → (3 + 2, 7 – 5) = (5, –7)

SYMMETRY AND TRANSFORMATION GEOMETRY – TYPICAL QUESTIONS

1 Find the vectors that translate: (a) (2, 3) to (7, 1)   (b) (–1, –3) to (–3, 3)

2 Find the images of these points under these rotations about the origin.
   (a) (5, 4), +90°   (b) (–4, –3), 180°   (c) (4, –3), +270°   (d) (–3, 4), –90°

3 Copy and complete these shaded shapes so that the lines AB are the lines of symmetry.

(a) 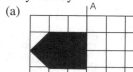   (b)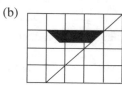

(c)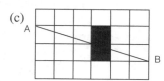

4 State the number of lines of symmetry and the order of rotational symmetry of each of these shapes:

(a)   (b)   (c)

(d)   (e)   (f)

5 Using graph paper or otherwise, find the images under the stated reflection of

(a) $(5, 4)$ in the x-axis (b) $(-3, -2)$ in the y-axis (c) $(5, -2)$ in line $y = 4$
(d) $(2, -5)$ in line $x = 5$ (e) $(-6, 1)$ in line $y = x$ (f) $(-5, -4)$ in line $y = -x$

6 Find the images of these points under these translations.

(a) $(4, -3)$ $\begin{pmatrix} 4 \\ 2 \end{pmatrix}$ (b) $(-1, 5)$ $\begin{pmatrix} -3 \\ 4 \end{pmatrix}$ (c) $(0, -5)$ $\begin{pmatrix} 3 \\ 2 \end{pmatrix}$ (d) $(-3, 4)$ $\begin{pmatrix} -5 \\ -4 \end{pmatrix}$

7 (a) What are the vectors of the translations that begin at each of A, B and C in this diagram?

(b) Write down the coordinates of the images of P $(-1, -2)$ under the three translations.

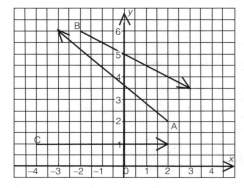

8 (a) On graph paper, draw the triangle ABC with A $(1, 1)$, B $(1, 3)$ and C $(3, 1)$.

(b) Copy and complete this table. Use it to draw the graph of $y = x + 4$.

x	1	2	3	4
$y = x + 4$				

(c) Reflect the triangle ABC in the line $y = x + 4$ and draw its image. Label it $A_1B_1C_1$.

(d) The triangle ABC is rotated through $180°$ about the origin. Draw the image and label it $A_2B_2C_2$.

(e) The triangle $A_2B_2C_2$ is translated by $\begin{pmatrix} 4 \\ -1 \end{pmatrix}$. Draw the image and label it $A_3B_3C_3$.

Unit 17 _____
CIRCLES

Circle vocabulary

The terms circumference, radius (plural radii) and diameter were revised in Unit 7.

A line across a circle that does not go through the centre is a **chord**. It divides the circle into two **segments**. The smaller segment is the **minor segment**. The larger segment is the **major segment**.

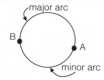

An **arc** is a part of the circumference of a circle. Two points A and B on the circumference divide the circumference into two arcs. The longer one is the **major arc**. The smaller one is the **minor arc**.

A **sector** is part of a circle that is bounded by two radii and an arc.

In this diagram, angle AOB is **subtended** by arc AB at the centre O, angle APB is subtended by arc AB at P.

A circle is named by the points on its circumference. The circle in this diagram is circle PQRS.

Angles and chords

Cut out a circle and draw a chord AB as shown in the diagram. O is the centre of the circle.

Fold the paper along the chord AB so that the points A and B are together. The line of the fold *m* bisects AB and goes through the centre, O.
The line of the fold is the perpendicular bisector of AB.

> **The perpendicular bisector of a chord of a circle goes through the centre of the circle.**

There is only one line that goes through O and is perpendicular to AB. This line bisects AB.

> **The perpendicular from the centre of a circle to a chord bisects the chord.**

In this diagram, length of chord AB = length of chord CD. If chord CD slides round the circle until C is on A, then D will be on B, because AB = CD. The two chords, AB and CD are the same distance from the centre O.

> **Equal chords of a circle are the same distance from the centre. Conversely, if two chords are the same distance from the centre, they must be the same length.**

Example A circle has a radius of 13 cm. How far from the centre is a chord of length 10 cm?

Start by drawing a diagram.
The chord is bisected by the perpendicular from the centre.
$\frac{1}{2}$ of 10 cm is 5 cm.
The triangle is right-angled, so Pythagoras' theorem can be used. (See Unit 18.)
$d^2 + 5^2 = 13^2$ so $d^2 = 13^2 - 5^2 = 169 - 25 = 144$ and $d = \sqrt{144}$
The distance is 12 cm.

Angles in circles

Angle at the centre of a circle

Draw a circle. Mark the centre O and three points A, Q and B on the circumference.
Join OA, OB, QA and QB. Measure $\angle AQB$ and $\angle AOB$.
You will find that $\angle AOB = 2 \times \angle AQB$.
$\angle AOB$ is the angle **subtended** by arc AB at O.
It can be proved that this is true for all points on all circles.

> **The angle subtended at the centre of a circle by an arc is twice the angle at the circumference subtended by the same arc.**

Angles in the same segment

In this diagram, P, Q and R are on the
circumference in the same segment of the circle.
∠AOB = 2∠AQB (from the previous result).
Also ∠AOB = 2∠APB
and ∠AOB = 2∠ARB
So ∠APB = ∠AQB = ∠ARB (each is $\frac{1}{2}$∠AOB)

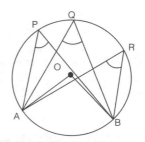

> **Angles subtended in the same segment of a circle from the
> same arc are equal.**

Example   In this diagram, ABCO is a rhombus.
∠APC = 50°. O is the centre of the circle. Find ∠ABC.
∠AOC = 2∠APC = 100° (angle at centre)
So ∠ABC = 100° (opposite angles of a rhombus are
            equal)

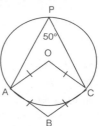

Angle in a semicircle

In this diagram, ∠AOB = 2∠ACB (the angle at the centre
is twice the angle at the circumference)
∠AOB makes a straight line so it is 180°.
So 2∠ACB = 180° and ∠ACB = 90°

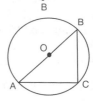

> **The angle in a semicircle is 90°.**

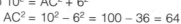

Example   In this diagram, AB is a diameter and O is the centre of the circle.

∠ABC = 21°. Calculate (a) ∠BAC   (b) ∠BCO
(c) f the radius is 5 cm and BC = 6 cm, how long is AC?

(a) ∠ACB = 90°, as AB is a diameter.
   So ∠BAC = 90° − 21° = 69°
(b) OB = OC (radii) so ∠BCO = ∠ABC = 21°
(c) Radius OB = 5 cm, so diameter AB = 10 cm.
   By Pythagoras' theorem, $AB^2 = AC^2 + BC^2$
                   so $10^2 = AC^2 + 6^2$
                      $AC^2 = 10^2 − 6^2 = 100 − 36 = 64$
   So AC = $\sqrt{64}$ cm = 8 cm

Cyclic quadrilaterals

A **cyclic quadrilateral** is a quadrilateral whose four
vertices are all on the circumference of a circle. Draw a
diagram like this one but larger.

Join BO and OD.
If ∠BAD = x then obtuse ∠BOD = 2x (angle at
the centre of a circle)
If ∠BCD = y, then reflex ∠BOD = 2y
Adding, 2x + 2y = reflex ∠BOD + obtuse ∠BOD
= 360°. So x + y = 180°

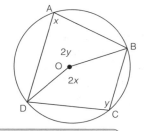

The opposite angles of a cyclic quadrilateral are supplementary.

Notice how these four results go together. The second, third and fourth all follow from the fact that the angle at the centre of a circle is twice the angle at
the circumference.

Tangents

This diagram shows a point P and a circle
centre O. Four lines are drawn from P.
Line PA does not touch the circle.
Line PBC cuts the circle at B and C.
Lines PS and PT touch the circle at one point.
The line PS and PT are **tangents** to the circle.
From any point outside a circle there are always two tangents to the circle.

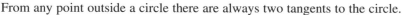

PX is a tangent of the circle centre O.
∠PXO = 90°.

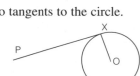

**A tangent to a circle is perpendicular to the radius drawn from the
point of contact to the centre.**

Now draw the other tangent from P to the circle. Label
the point Y where the tangent touches the circle.
Measure the lengths of PX and PY.
They are equal.
This can be proved as follows. Look at triangles PXO and PYO.
    OX = OY (radii)
∠PXO = ∠PYO = 90° (radii perpendicular to tangents)
PO is common to both triangles.
So triangles PXO and PYO are congruent (RHS) and PX = PY.

The two tangents from a point to a circle are equal in length.

Also ∠OPX = ∠OPY (corresponding angles of the two congruent triangles) and so PO bisects ∠XPY, the angle between the tangents.

> **The line joining an external point to the centre of a circle bisects the angle between the tangents from the point to the circle.**

Example XP and XQ are tangents 8 cm long to the circle in the diagram. QR is the 6 cm long diameter of the circle. ∠PQR = 20°

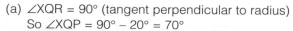

Find (a) ∠XQP (b) ∠PXQ (c) the length XR

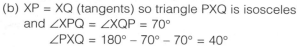

(a) ∠XQR = 90° (tangent perpendicular to radius)
So ∠XQP = 90° − 20° = 70°
(b) XP = XQ (tangents) so triangle PXQ is isosceles
and ∠XPQ = ∠XQP = 70°
∠PXQ = 180° − 70° − 70° = 40°
(c) Triangle XRQ is right angled (tangent perpendicular to radius).
By Pythagoras' theorem, $XR^2 = 8^2 + 6^2$
$= 64 + 36 = 100$
so XR = 10 cm

CIRCLES – TYPICAL QUESTIONS

Give answers to 3 significant figures where appropriate.

1 How far is a chord 14 cm long from the centre of a circle radius 24 cm?

2 How long is a chord that is 15 cm from the centre of a circle radius 25 cm?

3 A circle has a radius of 12 cm. Two chords of length 16 cm and 20 cm are parallel. How far apart are they? (There are two possible answers.)

4 A chord 20 cm long is 12 cm from the centre of a circle. What is the radius of the circle?

5 ABCD is a cyclic quadrilateral. BAE is a straight line. ∠BCD = 88° and ∠ADC = 121°. Calculate (a) ∠ABC (b) ∠EAD.

6 WXYZ is a cyclic quadrilateral. WX and ZY produced meet at A. ∠WAZ = 40°. ∠XYA = 75°. Find the angles of the cyclic quadrilateral.

7 ABCD is a cyclic quadrilateral. AB is a diameter of the circle. ∠CAB = 29°. ∠DBA = 41°. Find ∠DAC.

8 PQ is the diameter of a circle. R is a point on the circumference of the circle.
(a) If ∠PQR = 68°, what is ∠QPR?
(b) If PQ = 12 cm and QR = 8 cm, how long is PR?

Unit 18 _____
PYTHAGORAS' THEOREM AND TRIGONOMETRY

Pythagoras' theorem and its converse

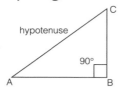

ABC is a right-angled triangle with $\angle ABC = 90°$.
The longest side is opposite the right angle.
This side is called the **hypotenuse**.

> **Pythagoras' theorem states that, in this right-angled triangle,**
> **$AB^2 + BC^2 = AC^2$.**

The converse of Pythagoras' theorem states that if $AB^2 + BC^2 = AC^2$ in triangle ABC, then the triangle is right-angled at B.

Pythagoras' theorem can be demonstrated by drawing a right-angled triangle, measuring the lengths of its sides, find their squares and adding the squares of the two smaller sides.

Applications of Pythagoras' theorem

Use Pythagoras' theorem to find the third side of a right-angled triangle when the other sides are known. Draw a diagram of the right-angled triangle. The side opposite the right angle is the hypotenuse, the longest side. Write out an equation using Pythagoras' theorem and then solve it.

Finding the hypotenuse when two shorter sides are known

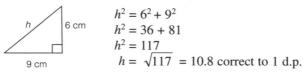

$h^2 = 6^2 + 9^2$
$h^2 = 36 + 81$
$h^2 = 117$
$h = \sqrt{117} = 10.8$ correct to 1 d.p.

Finding the third side when the hypotenuse and one other side are known

$x^2 + 24^2 = 25^2$
$x^2 + 576 = 625$
$x^2 = 625 - 576 = 49$
$x = \sqrt{49} = 7$

When you have your answer – check that it is sensible. The hypotenuse should be longer than the other two sides – but not too much longer. The other sides should be shorter than the hypotenuse.

For problems without a diagram, **start by making a sketch**. Mark the sides and angles that you are given. Then carry on as above.

Example 1   A rectangle is 8 m by 10 m.

How long are the diagonals, to 1 decimal place?

Draw a diagram.

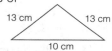

If d is the length of the diagonal, $d^2 = 10^2 + 8^2$
$$d^2 = 100 + 64 = 164$$
$$d = \sqrt{164} = 12.8 \text{ to 1 d.p.}$$

The diagonals are 12.8 m long, to 1 decimal place.

Example 2   An isosceles triangle has sides of 13 cm, 13 cm and 10 cm. What is its area?

Draw a diagram.

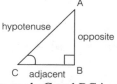

The area $= \frac{1}{2}$ base × height. To find the height, divide the isosceles triangle down the middle into 2 right-angled triangles. The base is bisected.

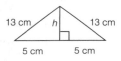

By Pythagoras' theorem, $5^2 + h^2 = 13^2$
$$h^2 = 13^2 - 5^2$$
$$= 169 - 25 = 144$$

So $h = \sqrt{144} = 12$. The height is 12 cm.

Area $= \frac{1}{2}$ base × height $= \frac{1}{2} \times 10 \times 12 = 60 \text{ cm}^2$

Tangent, sine and cosine ratios

In a right-angled triangle, the **opposite side** is the one opposite the angle being used. The **adjacent side** is the one next to the angle.

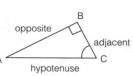

In both diagrams, AB is opposite angle C and BC is adjacent to angle C. BC is opposite angle A and AB is adjacent to angle A. AC is the hypotenuse. The sine, cosine and tangent ratios of angles in right-angled triangles are:

$$\text{sine } D = \frac{\text{opposite}}{\text{hypotenuse}} = \frac{EF}{DE}$$

$$\text{cosine } D = \frac{\text{adjacent}}{\text{hypotenuse}} = \frac{DF}{DE}$$

$$\text{tangent } D = \frac{\text{opposite}}{\text{adjacent}} = \frac{EF}{DF}$$

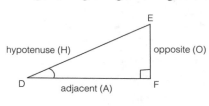

In brief, $\sin D = \dfrac{O}{H}$, $\cos D = \dfrac{A}{H}$, $\tan D = \dfrac{O}{A}$

> **Finding sin, cos and tan of an angle using a calculator**
> For example, to find sin 58°, press **sin 58** and read 0.8480481.
> The answer is 0.848 to 3 significant figures.
> Similarly, to find cos 58°, press **cos 58**; to find tan 58°, press **tan 58**.
>
> To find the angle whose cos is 0.54, use INVERSE:
> press **INV cos 0.54 =** and read 57.316361. The answer is 57.3° to 3 s.f.
> **Do not leave the answer with many decimal places.**
> Follow a similar procedure to find the angle when the sine or tangent
> is given.

Using the tangent

Use the tangent ratio to solve problems in right-angled triangles that involve
the two shorter sides.

Example 1   In this triangle, AG = 2 cm and AF = 3 cm.
∠GAF = 90°. Find ∠AGF and ∠AFG.

$\tan \angle AGF = \frac{3}{2}$ so ∠AGF = 56.3° to 1 d.p.

∠AFG = 90° − 56.3° = 33.7°, correct to 1 d.p.

Example 2   In this triangle, ∠PQR = 90° and
QRP = 38°. PQ = 15 cm. Find the length of QR.

$\tan 38° = \dfrac{15}{QR}$

so $QR = \dfrac{15}{\tan 38°} = 19.2$ cm to 3 s.f.

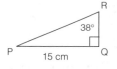

[When working out this problem on a calculator, press tan [15 ÷ 38] = .
There is no need to write down the value of tan 38°.]

Using the sine

Use the sine ratio to solve problems in right-angled triangles that involve the
opposite side and the hypotenuse.

Example 1   A plank 7 m long leans against a vertical wall 5 m high.
Find the angle between the plank and the horizontal ground.

Draw a diagram.
AC is the 7 m plank and AB is the 5 m wall. ∠B = 90°.
The questions asks what angle C is.

$\sin C = \dfrac{Opp}{Hyp} = \dfrac{5}{7}$ and ∠C = 45.6 , correct to 1 d.p.

108

Example 2   A car travels 8 km from the bottom to the top of a hill along a straight road inclined at 5° to the horizontal. Calculate the height of the hill, giving your answer to the nearest metre.

Draw a diagram to show this information.
On the diagram, the height of the hill is h.

$$\sin 5° = \frac{\text{Opp}}{\text{Hyp}} = \frac{h}{8}$$

so $h = 8 \sin 5° = 0.697$ km $= 697$ m, correct to 3 s.f.

Using the cosine

Use the cosine ratio to solve problems in right-angled triangles that involve the adjacent side and the hypotenuse.

Example 1   A straight rope is attached to the ground from the top of a flag-pole. The bottom of the rope is 20 m from the base of the flag-pole, and the rope makes an angle of 54° with the ground. How long is the rope?

Start with a diagram.

$$\sin 54° = \frac{\text{Adj}}{\text{Hyp}} = \frac{20}{r} \text{ so } r = \frac{20}{\cos 54°} = 34.0$$

The rope is 34.0 m long.

In the exam, you will have to decide which ratio (sin, cos or tan) to use in each question.

Example 2   Find x, correct to 3 s.f.

There is no right angle in the diagram.
The triangle is isosceles. Cut it down the middle into 2 right-angled triangles.

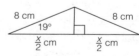

Look at one right-angled triangle.
You know the angle and the hypotenuse
and you are asked for the adjacent side. So cos must be used.

$$\cos 19° = \frac{x/2}{8} = \frac{x}{16}$$

$x = 16 \cos 19° = 15.1$ to 3 significant figures.

Angle of elevation and depression

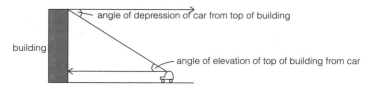

The angle of depression is **downwards** from the horizontal.

The angle of elevation is **upwards** from the horizontal.

Angle of elevation = Angle of depression

The tangent ratio is often used to find lengths and heights in problems involving angles of elevation or depression.

Example 1   Masli is standing 40 m from a tree. He measures the angle of elevation of the top of the tree and finds that it is 36°. Masli is 1.75 m tall. How tall is the tree?

Start with a diagram.
Remember to allow for Masli's height.
If the tree is h m tall, the top of the tree is $(h - 1.75)$ m taller than Masli.

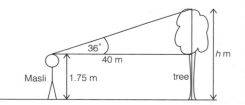

$$\tan 36° = \frac{\text{Opp}}{\text{Adj}} = \frac{h - 1.75}{40}$$
$$h - 1.75 = 40 \tan 36°$$
$$h = 1.75 + 40 \tan 36° = 30.81$$

The tree is 30.8 m tall, to 3 significant figures.

Example 2   The angle of depression of an object on the ground from the top of a building is 40°. The building is 30 m tall. What is the horizontal distance of the object from the base of the building? Give your answer to 3 s.f.

Use the fact that the angle of elevation is the same as the angle of depression.

$$\tan 40° = \frac{\text{Opp}}{\text{Adj}} = \frac{30}{d}$$
$$d = \frac{30}{\tan 40°} = 35.8 \text{ m}$$

The distance of the object from the building is 35.8 m, to 3 s.f.

EXAM TIP

Solving trigonometry and Pythagoras problems in Paper 1
In Paper 1 no calculators are allowed. This means that
a. Pythagoras problems have to work out nicely.
   For example, if you work out that $x^2 = 12^2 - 5^2 = 144 - 25 = 119$ and
   $x = \sqrt{119}$, you have probably made a mistake, as you need a calculator
   to work out $\sqrt{119}$.
b. It is useful to learn the **squares** of important numbers off by heart:

11^2	12^2	13^2	14^2	15^2	16^2	17^2	18^2	19^2	20^2
121	144	169	196	225	256	289	324	361	400

c. The sin, cos and tan of all the angles you need in trigonometry
   questions must be given.

Example 3   In the diagram, B = 90°, A = 50° and AC = 6 cm.
Given that sin 50° = 0.766, cos 50° = 0.643 and
tan 50° = 1.19, find the length of AB.

AB is adjacent to ∠A so use cosine:

$$\cos 50° = \frac{\text{Adj}}{\text{Hyp}} = \frac{\text{AB}}{6}$$

so AB = 6 × 0.643 cm = 3.858 cm

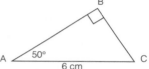

PYTHAGORAS' THEOREM AND TRIGONOMETRY – TYPICAL QUESTIONS

1 For each figure, find the value of x.

(a) 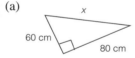   (b)   (c)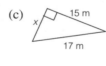

2 A rectangle is 12 m by 9 m. Find the length of a diagonal.

3 x is an acute angle.
   (a) If cos x = 0.234, find x, correct to 2 decimal places.
   (b) If sin x = 0.5432, find x, correct to 3 decimal places.
   (c) If tan x = 1.8, find x, correct to the nearest whole number.

4 For each of these diagrams, find the values of x and y.

(a) 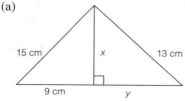   (b)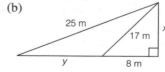

5 In the diagram, PQR is a triangle and QS is perpendicular to PR. PQ = 13 cm, PS = 5 cm and SR = 9 cm.
Calculate   (a) the length of QR
            (b) cos ∠QRS

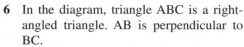

6 In the diagram, triangle ABC is a right-angled triangle. AB is perpendicular to BC.
AB = 12 cm and BC = 16 cm.
(a) Calculate the length of AC.
(b) ∠BDC = 90°. Calculate the length of BD.
(c) Calculate sin ∠ACB.

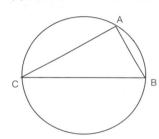

7

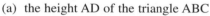

In the diagram, BC is a diameter of the circle. The radius of the circle is 8 cm. AB = 12 cm.
(a) Calculate AC.
(b) Calculate the area of triangle ABC.
(c) Calculate angle ABC.
Give your answers to 3 significant figures.

8 In the diagram, the base BC of isosceles triangle ABC is 8 cm long and the angle ABC is 76°;
sin 76° = 0.970, cos 76° = 0.242, tan 76° = 4.01.
Without using a calculator, find
(a) the height AD of the triangle ABC
(b) the area of triangle ABC.

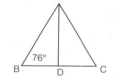

9 In the diagram, ADC is a straight line. Given that ∠BAD = 50°, AB = 40 cm and DC = 50 cm, calculate
(a) the length of BD, correct to 3 s.f.
(b) the angle x, correct to the nearest degree.

10 In the diagram, a man looks out of a window of building A and looks at building B. The angle of elevation of the top of building B is 45° and the angle of depression of the foot of building B is 30°.

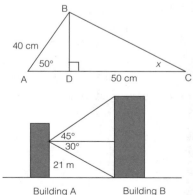

The eye level of the man is 21 m above the ground.
(a) Calculate the horizontal distance between the buildings, correct to the nearest metre.
(b) Calculate the height of the building B, correct to the nearest metre.
(c) A radio mast 20 m tall is put on building B. What is the angle of elevation of the top of the mast from the man, correct to the nearest degree?

11 The diagram illustrates a solid cone. The radius of the base of the cone is 6.5 cm, the height of the cone is 18 cm.

Calculate
(a) the area of the base of the cone
(b) the volume of the cone
(c) the length of the slant side of the cone
(d) the area of the curved surface of the cone.
(Take π to be 3.14 and give your answers to 3 significant figures.)

12 In the diagram, VWXYZ is a rectangular pyramid. WX = 8 cm and the area of WXYZ = 48 cm^2.
(a) Find the length of WZ.
(b) Find the length of WY.
(c) If VO = 12 cm, find VY.
(d) Name a triangle that is congruent to $\triangle$ VOX.

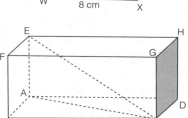

13 The diagram shows a cuboid.
The length of AC is 17 cm and BC is 15 cm. Find
(a) the length of AB ($\angle$ABC is a right angle)
(b) the length of AE if the volume of the cuboid is 600 cm^3
(c) the total surface area of the cuboid.

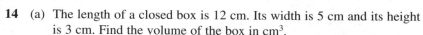

14 (a) The length of a closed box is 12 cm. Its width is 5 cm and its height is 3 cm. Find the volume of the box in cm^3.
(b) Only the four sides of the box are painted; the top and the bottom of the box are not painted. Find the total area of the box that is painted.

Unit 19
INTRODUCTION TO STATISTICS

Statistics are about **data** (information) – its collection, organisation, representation on diagrams and interpretation.

Collecting data

When collecting data, use **data collection sheets** or **tally charts**. The data can be recorded using **tally marks** ////. The fifth tally mark is drawn across the first four: ////. Counting the tally marks in each row of the chart gives the frequency of each category. Frequency means 'how many'. By listing the frequencies in a column, a **frequency table** is formed.

Example A student carried out a survey to find out how her fellow students travelled to school. This is what she found:

Walk	Bicycle	Car	Bus	Car	Bicycle	Walk	Bus	Car
Walk	Walk	Car	Walk	Walk	Walk	Car	Car	Walk
Car	Walk	Walk	Car	Walk	Bus	Walk	Car	Bus
Car	Walk	Walk	Walk	Bus	Car	Bus	Walk	Walk
Bus	Walk	Car	Walk	Walk	Car	Walk	Bus	Walk
Bus	Walk	Walk	Walk	Walk	Walk	Car	Car	Car
Car	Car	Car	Car	Bicycle	Bicycle			

Her tally table looked like this:

Travel	Tallies	Total
Walk	//// //// //// //// //// //	27
Car	//// //// //// ////	20
Bus	//// ////	9
Bicycle	////	4
	Total	60

The frequency table looked like this:

Travel	Walk	Car	Bus	Bicycle	Total
Total	27	20	9	4	60

114

Data representation

There are several ways that data in frequency tables can be displayed. You may be expected to look at diagrams and interpret them or to show data in diagrams.

Pie charts

A pie chart uses sectors of a circle to compare the different quantities in a table. The angle of each sector is proportional to the quantity that it illustrates.

The angle of each sector is $\dfrac{\text{Quantity shown by sector}}{\text{Total quantity}} \times 360°$.

The angles for the example above are:

Travel	Total	Angle
Walk	27	$\dfrac{27}{60} \times 360° = 162°$
Car	20	$\dfrac{20}{60} \times 360° = 120°$
Bus	9	$\dfrac{9}{60} \times 360° = 54°$
Bicycle	4	$\dfrac{4}{60} \times 360° = 24°$
Total	60	360°

The angles of the sectors must add up to 360°.

The **pie chart** looks like this:

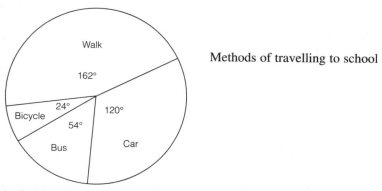

Methods of travelling to school

A pie chart is a good way of comparing quantities. The circle represents the total; the relative sizes of the parts show up well.

Pictograms

A **pictogram** uses pictures to represent quantities of an item. The quantities are proportional to the number of pictures or to the size of the pictures. For the information above, there could be 27 pictures of walkers, 20 cars, 9 buses and 4 bicycles.

Bar graphs

There are two forms of bar graph: horizontal and vertical. Each bar has the same width.

The table on the previous page can be shown on a **vertical bar graph**:

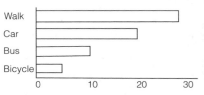

Or on a **horizontal bar graph**:

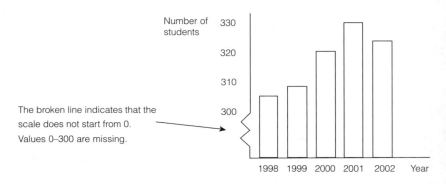

Sometimes the vertical scale does not start from 0. For example, the number of students in a school were as follows:

Year	1998	1999	2000	2001	2002
Number of students	305	310	320	330	325

This can be shown on a bar graph starting from 300:

The broken line indicates that the scale does not start from 0. Values 0–300 are missing.

116

Line graphs

The last graph can also be shown as a **line graph**:

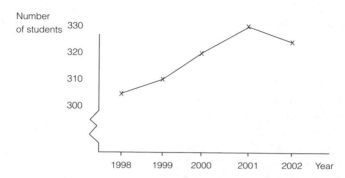

A line graph shows trends and changes between quantities over a period of time, e.g. body temperature, profits and losses. It is drawn by joining the midpoints of the tops of a column graph by straight lines. Line graphs should be drawn on graph paper.

Histograms

Histograms are similar to vertical bar graphs, but they are not the same. A histogram is used to represent continuous or grouped data. The area of each column represents the frequency that corresponds to a class. The length of each bar is proportional to the given quantities to allow for easy comparison.

The students in a class were asked how far they travelled to school each day. The distances were as follows:

Distance (km)	0–	1–	2–	3–	4–	5–	6–7
Number of students	4	7	6	5	4	2	3

This information can be shown on a **histogram**:

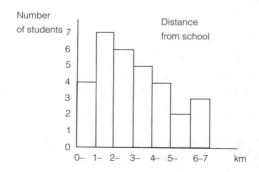

117

Mean, mode and median

The idea of an average is very useful, because it enables us to compare one set of data with another set by comparing just two numbers – their averages. There are three different averages you need to know about: **mean, median** and **mode**.

Mode

The **mode** is the most common score that occurs in a set of data. It is the value with the **highest frequency**. For example, what is the mode of the scores 4, 7, 8, 4, 6, 9, 9, 3, 7, 6, 7?
Look for the most common score. Looking at the scores, observe that 7 occurs three times, more than any other, so 7 is the mode.
The mode is a useful average because it is very easy to find. It can be found for non-numerical data. For example, most popular cars in Brunei for a particular year, the most popular colour, and so on.

Example What is the mode of 14, 17, 14, 16, 15, 13 and 16?

Two scores, 14 and 16, are the most common scores. There are two modes, 14 and 16. A set of numbers is said to be **bimodal** if it contains two modes.

Remember that the **mode is not the frequency** of the most common score or scores. The mode is always a score (or scores).

Median

The **median** of a set of numbers is the **middle** value of the scores after they have been **put in order** of size, from lowest to highest.
What is the median of 14, 17, 14, 16, 15, 13 and 16? **First put them in order.**
In order these numbers are 13, 14, 14, **15**, 16, 16 and 17. The median is the score in the middle, which is 15. There are 3 scores more than it and 3 scores less than it.
The next example shows how to find the **median of an even number of scores.**

Example What is the median of 1, 2, 2, 3, 3, 4, 5, 6, 7, 8?

There are 10 scores altogether.
The scores divide into two halves 1, 2, 2, 3, 3 and 4, 5, 6, 7, 8.
The two middle scores are the 5th and 6th terms, which are 3 and 4.
The median is the mean of these two middle scores, which is $\dfrac{3+4}{2} = \dfrac{7}{2} = 3.5$

The median of n numbers arranged in order is the $\dfrac{n+1}{2}$ th term.

So for 105 terms, the median is the $\dfrac{105 + 1}{2} = \dfrac{106}{2} = 53$rd term in order.

The median of 106 terms is the $\dfrac{106 + 1}{2} = \dfrac{107}{2} = 53\frac{1}{2}$th term. This is the mean of the 53rd and 54th terms.

The advantage of using the median as an average is that half the scores are less than or equal to the median value and half are more than or equal to it. Therefore, the average is only slightly affected by the presence of any particularly high or low values that are not typical of the data as a whole.

Mean

The **mean** of a set of values is the total of all the values in the set divided by the total number of values in the set:

$$\textbf{Mean} = \frac{\text{Sum of all the values}}{\text{Total number of values}}$$

This is what most people mean when they use the term 'average'.

Example 1   The marks out of 10 of the students in a class in a mathematics test were:

Boys: 6, 2, 2, 5, 7, 6, 2, 8, 7

Girls: 4, 6, 7, 2, 5, 7, 9, 6, 8, 7.   Who did better, the boys or the girls?

The mean score of the boys is:

$$\frac{\text{The sum of their scores}}{\text{The number of boys}} = \frac{6 + 2 + 2 + 5 + 7 + 6 + 2 + 8 + 7}{9} = \frac{45}{9} = 5.0$$

The mean score of the girls is:

$$\frac{\text{The sum of their scores}}{\text{The number of girls}} = \frac{4 + 6 + 7 + 2 + 5 + 7 + 9 + 6 + 8 + 7}{10} = \frac{61}{10} = 6.1$$

The girls had a higher mean score.

The mean of scores can also be calculated from a frequency table. This is the frequency table of the boys' scores:

Score (x)	Frequency (f)	Frequency × score $(f\,x)$
2	3	6
5	1	5
6	2	12
7	2	14
8	1	8
Total	9	45

The mean score = $\dfrac{45}{9}$ = 5

This is quicker than writing out all the scores and adding them together.

The advantage of using the mean as average is that it takes into account all the values in the set of data.

> **The mode is the MOST COMMON score.**
> **The mean is TOTAL of scores ÷ number of scores.**
> **The median is the MIDDLE score when the scores are in order.**

Example 2   This frequency table shows the number of goals a football team scored in each match of a season. Find the mode, mean and median for the number of goals scored.

No. of goals	Frequency
0	2
1	4
2	8
3	10
4	6

The mode is the one with the highest frequency. The mode is 3.
There are 2 + 4 + 8 + 10 + 6 = 30 matches. The median is the average of the 15th and 16th scores, arranged in order.
In order, the first 2 scores are 0, the next 4 scores are 1 and the next 8 scores are 2.
That is 14 scores: 0, 0, 1, 1, 1, 1, 2, 2, 2, 2, 2, 2, 2, 2 so far. The next 10 in the list are all 3, so the 15th and 16th scores are both 3. The median is 3.
The mean is $\dfrac{0 \times 2 + 1 \times 4 + 2 \times 8 + 3 \times 10 + 4 \times 6}{30} = \dfrac{74}{30}$ = 2.5 to 1 d.p.

INTRODUCTION TO STATISTICS – TYPICAL QUESTIONS

1   Find the mean, median and mode of each of these sets of scores.
   (a) 5, 5, 7, 8, 9   (b) 4, 6, 7, 9, 10, 10

2   The frequency table shows the marks (out of 10) obtained by students in a spelling test.

Mark	3	4	5	6	7	8	9	10
Frequency	1	2	6	5	5	4	3	4

   (a) Write down the modal mark.
   (b) What is the mean of the marks obtained by the students?

3 A group of 10 students had lunch in a restaurant. Here are the amounts that each of them spent: $2.30, $2.20, $2.50, $2.20, $2.50, $2.20, $2.20, $2.30, $2.40, $2.20

Find the mode, median and mean of these prices.

4 A six-sided die is thrown 29 times. The results are shown in this table.

Number shown on die	1	2	3	4	5	6
Frequency	8	7	5	2	3	4

(a) For these results, write down (i) the mode   (ii) the median.
(b) The die is thrown one more time. Find the number shown on the die if the mean of 30 throws is to be exactly 3.

5 This pie chart shows the distribution of population in a village.

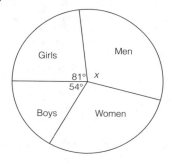

(a) Calculate the percentage of the population who are girls.
(b) Given that there are twice as many women as men, calculate x.
(c) If the number of boys is 432, calculate the total population of the village.

6 Tickets for a show cost $1, $2, $5 or $20. The number of tickets sold were as follows:

Price	$1	$2	$5	$20
Number of tickets sold	84	68	22	6

(a) Write down the modal price.
(b) Find the median price.
(c) Draw a pie chart to show the number of tickets sold at each price.

7 The table shows the population of a town, rounded to the nearest thousand, after each census.
(a) Draw a line graph for the data.

Year	1941	1951	1961	1971	1981	1991	2001
Population (1000s)	12	14	15	18	21	25	23

(b) From your graph, estimate the population in 1965.
(c) Between which two consecutive censuses did the population increase the most?

ANSWERS

Unit 2
1. (a) 2 (b) 70 (c) 60 (d) 22 (e) −4 (f) 71
2. (a) (i) 80 (ii) 60 (iii) 72
   (b) (i) 6 (ii) 20 (iii) 1
3. (a) The answers are all the same (192)
   (b) The answers are all the same (360)
4. (a) 32 761 (b) 4913 (c) 4096 (d) 6561 (e) 399
5. (a) 15 (b) 2 (c) −2 (d) 1 (e) 24 (f) 15
6. (a) 1 (b) 2 (c) 10 (d) −36 (e) 16 (f) 12
7. (a) < (b) = (c) = (d) < (e) > (f) >

Unit 3
1. Three of (a) $^4/_{10}$, $^6/_{15}$, $^8/_{20}$, $^{10}/_{25}$, ...
   (b) $^{12}/_{21}$, $^{16}/_{28}$, $^8/_{14}$, $^{20}/_{35}$, ...
   (c) $^6/_{20}$, $^9/_{30}$, $^{12}/_{40}$, $^{15}/_{50}$, ...
   (d) $^{12}/_{22}$, $^{18}/_{33}$, $^{24}/_{44}$, $^{30}/_{55}$, ...
   (e) $^3/_7$, $^9/_{21}$, $^{12}/_{28}$, $^{15}/_{35}$, ...
   (f) $^7/_9$, $^{14}/_{18}$, $^{28}/_{36}$, $^{35}/_{45}$, ...
2. (a) $^1/_2$ (b) $^3/_4$ (c) $^2/_5$ (cannot be simplified) (d) $^3/_4$ (e) $^3/_7$ (f) $^1/_4$
3. (a) > (b) > (c) < (d) <
4. (a) $1^{13}/_{15}$ (b) $1^1/_5$ (c) $2^2/_5$ (d) $7^1/_6$ (e) $6^3/_4$ (f) $2^1/_2$
5. (a) $3^2/_3$ (b) $^{17}/_{20}$ (c) $^6/_{35}$ (d) $2^1/_{15}$ (e) $1^1/_{10}$ (f) $1^5/_6$
6. (a) $51^5/_6$ (b) $92^1/_{12}$ (c) $41^4/_{15}$ (d) $33^5/_8$ (e) $117^7/_{12}$ (f) $^1/_2$
7. (a) $16^2/_3$ (b) $25^1/_4$ (c) $73^3/_8$ (d) $76^3/_8$
8. (a) $^1/_4$ (b) $^1/_5$ (c) $^2/_3$ (d) 4 (e) $^{14}/_{33}$
9. (a) 0.2 (b) 0.55 (c) 0.425 (d) 0.666...

10. (a) 12.5; 10.5; 0.00406; 2000
    (b) 43; 6.5; 280 000; 2000
    (c) 2.0; 12.6; 4.6; 2.0
    (d) 456.79; 0.01; 2.00
11. (a) 40 (b) 680 (c) 4.29
    (d) 4.25 (e) 984 000 (f) 0.00423

Unit 4
1. (a) (i) 70% (ii) 52% (iii) 90%
   (b) (i) 0.78 (ii) 0.045 (iii) 2.45
   (c) (i) 45% (ii) 250% (iii) 5.6%
   (d) (i) $^7/_8$ (ii) $^{11}/_{40}$ (iii) $2^3/_4$
2. (a) 400 (b) 1.5%
3. (a) $180 (b) $40
4. 1350 girls
5. (a) B$391 (b) US$529.41
6. $10 300
7. $240
8. $200
9. (a) M$7200 (b) B$1280

Unit 5
1. (a) 2000 (b) 0.25 or $^1/_4$ (c) 48 (d) 513
2. (a) $5^1/_2$ (b) $1^2/_3$ (c) 1.5 (d) $1^4/_5$ (e) 36 (f) 22 (g) 120 (h) 30
3. 12.6
4. (a) 4^{12} (b) 4^9 (c) 2^{15} (d) 5^2 (e) 12^4 (f) 5^9 (g) $^1/_9$ (h) $^1/_6$ (i) 1 (j) 2^8 or 256 (k) $^1/_9$ (l) 3^{-5}
5. (a) 37 000 (b) 2 132 000 (c) 0.0345 (d) 0.6
6. (a) 8.166×10^6 (b) 5×10^2 (c) 8×10^7
7. (a) 3.5×10^3 (b) 2.84×10^0 (c) 1.54×10^4 (d) 4.98×10^5 (e) 7×10^6 (f) 4.76×10^{-2} (g) 5×10^9 (h) 5.7502×10^6
8. (a) 63 000 (b) 0.058 (c) 92 230 (d) 564 000 (e) 0.0064 (f) 62 400 000

9 (a) 8×10^{10} (b) 2×10^{1}
   (c) 3.2×10^{5} (d) 1.8×10^{10}

Unit 6
1 $2.70
2 $12
3 3 kg
4 (a) $10.50   (b) $9.45
5 (a) 1200 g   (b) 450 g
   (c) 1500 g
6 58 km
7 9.45 a.m.
8 (a) $7 : 5$ (b) $1 : 3$
9 (a) $1 : 40$ (b) $4 : 1$ (c) $8 : 1$
10 (a) $150; $200; $300
   (b) 50 cents; $1.00; $2.50
   (c) 25 cm; 35 cm; 40 cm
11 $24
12 $14 000
13 200 kg
14 $x = 3$
15 750 girls; 37.5% are boys
16 6 sweets

Unit 7
1 (a) 8 cm   (b) 6.5 cm   (c) 4.8 cm
2 (a) 4500 m   (b) 2850 m
   (c) 6.5 m
3 32 cm
4 (a) 125.6 cm   (b) 157 cm
   (c) 176 cm   (d) 2.2 cm
5 (a) 2000 km   (b) 14 m
6 11 cm
7 $^{1000}/_{80} = 12.5$ g/cm^3
8 (a) 0.834 kg   (b) 12 000 g
   (c) 2500 g   (d) 5.8 g   (e) 5800 g
   (f) 4.56 t
9 (a) 17.5%   (b) 5%   (c) $^4/_{15}$
10 2.20 p.m.
11 1 h 25 min
12 (a) 2 m   (b) 72 cm   (c) 44 cm
   (d) 2.32 m   (e) 16%

Unit 8
1 (a) 40 cm^2 (b) 21 cm^2 (c) 25 m^2
   (d) 120 cm^2
2 (a) 3 cm   (b) 12 cm   (c) 12 cm
   (d) 5 cm
3 (a) $4 : 7$ (b) $25 : 9$ (c) 125 cm^2
4 2510 cm^2
5 216 cm^2
6 1000 tiles

Unit 9
1 33 cm^2
2 (a) 150 m^3 (b) 190 cm^2
   (c) 112.5 cm^3
3 (a) 314 cm^2 (b) 1257 cm^3
4 160 cm^3
5 (a) 314 cm^3 (b) 282.6 cm^2
6 (a) 113 cm^2; 113 cm^3
   (b) 757 cm^2; 1050 cm^3
   (c) 1000 cm^2; 2000 cm^3
   (d) 7.85 cm^2; 1.57 cm^3

Unit 10
1 (a) $x + 6$ (b) $p - 12$ (c) $8x^2$
   (d) $^3/_4 y$ (e) $x + y$ (f) $(pq)^2$
2 (a) $8xy + x - 5y$ (b) $x + 5y$
   (c) $4x^2 - x + 4$ (d) $2m$
   (e) $6ab + 2bc + ac$
3 (a) -7 (b) 20   (c) -10 (d) 24
   (e) -12 (f) 91
4 (a) -3 (b) -2 (c) -6 (d) -30
   (e) 25   (f) -21
5 (a) 8   (b) -3 (c) -6 (d) 5   (e)
   -2 (f) 4
6 (a) 6   (b) 2   (c) $1^1/_2$ (d) 4   (e)
   -1 (f) 2
7 (a) 6   (b) 1   (c) -2 (d) 5
   (e) 2   (f) -3

Unit 11
1 (a) $5a + 10b$ (b) $x^2 - xy$
   (c) $2x^3 + 6x^2 - 2x$
   (d) $6x^3 - 10x^2 + 2x$
2 (a) $4x - 16y$ (b) $8c - 13$
   (c) $3x + 4$
3 (a) $x^2 + 5x - 24$ (b) $2x^2 + 11x - 6$
   (c) $12x^2 - 9xy - 3y^2$
   (d) $x^2 - 14x + 49$
   (e) $4x^2 + 20x + 25$
   (f) $16x^2 - 8x + 1$
4 (a) $x^2 - 9$ (b) $4y^2 - 16$
   (c) $25x^2 - 9y^2$
5 (a) $12x^2 - 4x$ (b) $6x + 3$
   (c) $x^2 + 3x - 12$
   (d) $3m^2 - 19mn + 7n^2$
6 (a) $5(a - 7)$ (b) $a(5a - 2)$
   (c) $3a(2b - 3a)$ (d) $5a(3bc + a)$
   (e) $3(2a + 3b - 4c)$ (f) $4(x + y - 3)$
   (g) $2x(4y - x + 3)$
   (h) $3a(x - 2y + 3z)$
7 (a) $-4, 1$ (b) $2, -20$ (c) $7, -6$
   (d) $(-6, -10)$

8 (a) $(x + 11)(x + 1)$
(b) $(x + 15)(x + 4)$
(c) $(x + 5)(x + 4)$
(d) $(x + 6)(x + 5)$
(e) $(x - 5)(x - 7)$
(f) $(x - 4)(x - 21)$
(g) $(x - 1)(x - 1)$
(h) $(x - 4)(x - 16)$
(i) $(x + 10)(x - 2)$
(j) $(x - 10)(x + 1)$
(k) $(x - 17)(x + 3)$
(l) $(x + 15)(x - 4)$
(m) $3(x + 2)(x - 2)$
(n) $4(x + 5)(x - 5)$
(o) $(ab + 11)(ab - 11)$
(p) $(3x + 5yz)(3x - 5yz)$

9 (a) $\dfrac{11}{2a}$ (b) $\dfrac{3c - 2b}{bc}$ (c) $\dfrac{7x + 1}{10}$

(d) $\dfrac{x + 12}{6}$ (e) $\dfrac{2x - 1}{x^2}$ (f) $\dfrac{3a}{5b}$

(g) $\dfrac{50z}{49p^2q^3}$ (h) $\dfrac{3x}{4}$

10 (a) $r = \pm\sqrt{\dfrac{A}{\pi h}}$ (b) $m = \dfrac{2E}{V^2}$

(c) $a = \dfrac{V - 3b}{2}$

11 $m = 1$

12 $r = \dfrac{2E - IR}{2I}$; $r = 3.5$

Unit 12

1 (a) $e = 4; f = 2$ (b) $c = 1; d = -4$
(c) $k = 3; n = \frac{1}{3}$ (d) $u = 1; v = 3$
2 (a) $e = 2; f = 1$ (b) $c = 1; d = -1$
(c) $e = 2; h = 3$ (d) $g = 3; h = -2$
3 (a) > (b) < (c) > (d) < (e) =
4 (a) $x < 2$ (b) $x \geq 4\frac{3}{5}$ (c) $y \leq 11$
(d) $x > 22$
(e) $y > 3$ (f) $x > -2$ (g) $x \leq 2$
(h) $x \geq 1$
5 (a)

(b)

(c)

(d)

6 $a + b = 180$, $a - b = 20$;
$a = 100$, $b = 80$
7 \$8.00 and \$6.00

Unit 13

1 (a) $\sqrt{40} = 6.32$ (b) $y = 3x - 4$
(c) 3
2 (a) $\sqrt{45} = 6.71$ (b) (8, 7.5)
(c) $x + 2y - 23 = 0$
3 (5, 6)
4 (a)

x	-2	-1	0	1	2
$y = 2x + 1$	-3	-1	1	3	5

(c) $x = 1$, $y = 3$
5 (a) $c = -4$ (b) Gradient is $\frac{1}{3}$;
y intercept is $(0, \frac{8}{3})$ (c) $y = 5$
6 (b) (i) \$22.05 (ii) 7 min
7 (b) The line is $y = \frac{1}{3}x$ (c) Points
could be (3, 1), (6, 2), (9, 3), …

Unit 14

1 (a) 240° (b) 54°
2 (a) $x = 32$ (b) $x = 45$, 48 or 60
3 $\angle CAB = 37°$, $\angle CBD = 112°$
4 $a = b = 70°$; $c = 110°$; $d = e = 140°$;
$f = 40°$
5 $x = 36°$, trapezium
6 (a) 18 sides (b) 40°
7 (a) 28° (b) 28°
8 (a) 36° (b) $n = 18$; 20°
9 15°
10 (a) 53° (b) 140°
(c) (i) 45° (ii) 135°

Unit 15

1 A and C are congruent; B, D and E
are congruent. All are equiangular
and therefore similar.
2 BA = BC; $\angle ADB = \angle CDB = 90°$;
DB is in both triangles which are
congruent (RHS).
3 (a) The triangles are equiangular.
As PQ//BC, $\angle AQP = \angle ABC$ and
$\angle APQ = \angle ACB$ (corresponding

angles equal). (b) (i) 15 cm
(ii) 2 : 3   (iii) 4 : 9
4 (a) The triangles are equiangular.
∠ADE = ∠ABC from the question.
∠A is a common angle.
(b) (i) 24 cm   (ii) 1 : 4
5 (a) 25 : 64   (b) 512 cm^2
6 (a) 5 : 4   (b) 8 cm
7 (a) 3 : 2   (b) 9 : 4   (c) 54 kg
8 (a) 16 km   (b) 20 cm   (c) 24 km^2
9 (a) 10 m   (b) 20 cm   (c) 5 cm^2

Unit 16

1 (a) $\begin{pmatrix} 5 \\ -2 \end{pmatrix}$ (b) $\begin{pmatrix} -2 \\ 6 \end{pmatrix}$

2 (a) (−4, 5)   (b) (4, 3)
(c) (−3, −4)   (d) (4, 3)
4 (a) Lines 1, order 1   (b) 0, 4
(c) 0, 2   (d) 5, 5   (e) 0, 2   (f) 2, 2
5 (a) (5, −4)   (b) (3, −2)   (c) (5, 10)
(d) (8, −5)   (e) (1, −6)   (f) (4, 5)
6 (a) (8, −1)   (b) (−4, 9)   (c) (3, −3)
(d) (−8, 0)

7 (a) $(2,2) \rightarrow (-3,6)$, A $= \begin{pmatrix} -5 \\ 4 \end{pmatrix}$;

$(-2,6) \rightarrow (3,3.5)$, B $= \begin{pmatrix} 5 \\ -2.5 \end{pmatrix}$;

$(-4,1) \rightarrow (2,1)$, C $= \begin{pmatrix} 6 \\ 0 \end{pmatrix}$

(b) (−6, 2), (4, −4.5), (5, −2)
8 (b)

x	1	2	3	4
$y = x + 4$	5	6	7	8

(c) A$_1$ = (−3, 5), B$_1$ = (−1, 5),
C$_1$ = (−3, 7)
(d) A$_2$ = (−1, −1), B$_2$ = (−1, −3),
C$_2$ = (−3, −1)
(e) A$_3$ = (3, −2), B$_3$ = (3, −4),
C$_3$ = (1, −2)

Unit 17

1 $\sqrt{24^2 - 7^2}$ cm = 23.0 cm

2 $2 \times \sqrt{25^2 - 15^2}$ cm = 40 cm

3 The chords are
$\sqrt{12^2 - 10^2}$ cm = 6.633 cm and
$\sqrt{12^2 - 8^2}$ cm = 8.944 cm from the
centre.

They are (6.633 + 8.944) cm = 15.6 cm
or (8.944 − 6.633) cm = 2.31 cm apart
(to 3 s.f.).
4 15.6 cm
5 (a) 59°   (b) 88°
6 ∠W = 75°, ∠X = 115°, ∠Y = 105°,
∠Z = 65°
7 20°
8 (a) 22° (b) $\sqrt{12^2 - 8^2}$ cm = 8.94 cm

Unit 18

1 (a) 100   (b) 8   (c) 8
2 $\sqrt{12^2 + 9^2}$ cm = 15 cm
3 (a) 76.47   (b) 32.902   (c) 61
4 (a) $x = 12$, $y = 5$
(b) $x = 15$, $y = 12$
5 (a) 15 cm   (b) $^9/_{15} = 0.6$
6 (a) 20 cm   (b) Area = $\frac{1}{2}$ BD × 20
= $\frac{1}{2}$ × 16 × 12 so BD = 9.6 cm
(c) 0.6

7 (a) $\sqrt{16^2 - 12^2}$ cm = 10.583 cm =
10.6 cm to 3 s.f.
(b) $\frac{1}{2}$ × 12 × 10.583 = 63.5 cm^2
(c) 41.4°

8 (a) AD/4 = tan 76° = 4.011 so AD =
16.044 cm
(b) $\frac{1}{2}$ × 8 × 16.044 = 64.176 cm^2
9 (a) 40 sin 50° = 30.6 cm   (b) 32°
10 (a) 36 m   (b) 57 m   (c) 57°
11 (a) 133 cm^2 (b) 796 cm^3 (c) 19.1
cm   (d) 391 cm^2 (using calculator)
12 (a) 6 cm   (b) 10 cm   (c) 13 cm
(d) ΔVOZ, ΔVOW or ΔVOY
13 (a) 8 cm   (b) 5 cm   (c) 470 cm^2
14 (a) 180 cm^3 (b) 102 cm^2

Unit 19

1 (a) Mean 6.8, median 7, mode 5
(b) Mean 7.7, median 8, mode 10
2 (a) 5   (b) 6.833
3 Mode $2.20, median $2.25, mean
$2.30
4 (a) (i) 1 (ii) 2   (b) 6
5 (a) 22.5%   (b) 75°   (c) 2880
6 (a) $1   (b) $2
(c) Angles are 168° ($1), 136° ($2),
44° ($5) and 12° ($20).
7 (b) 16 or 17 thousand
(c) 1961 and 1971

Macmillan Education Ltd
Between Towns Road, Oxford OX4 3PP
A division of Macmillan Publishers Limited
Companies and representatives throughout the world

ISBN 0 333 95095 X

First published 2004

Design by Wendy Bann
Typeset by EXPO Holdings
Illustrated by typesetter
Cover design by Jim Weaver Design
Cover photograph by John Suffolk

Printed and bound in Malaysia

2008 2007 2006 2005 2004
10 9 8 7 6 5 4 3 2 1